ELVIS | ULTIMATE C

ISBN 978-1-4234-4576-0

HAL•LEONARD®
CORPORATION
7777 W. BLUEMOUND RD. P.O. BOX 13819 MILWAUKEE, WI 53213

www.elvis.com

Visit Hal Leonard Online at
www.halleonard.com

HOW GREAT THOU ART

Words and Music by
STUART K. HINE

birds sing sweet-ly in the trees.____ When I look down from loft-y moun-tain
home, what joy shall fill my heart.____ Then I shall bow in hum-ble ad-o-

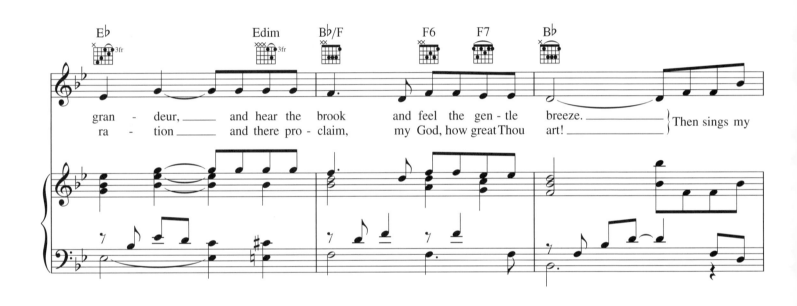

gran - deur,____ and hear the brook and feel the gen-tle breeze.____ } Then sings my
ra - tion____ and there pro - claim, my God, how great Thou art!____

soul, my Sav-iour God to Thee;_____ how great Thou

art, _____ how great Thou art! _____ Then sings my soul, my Sav-iour God to

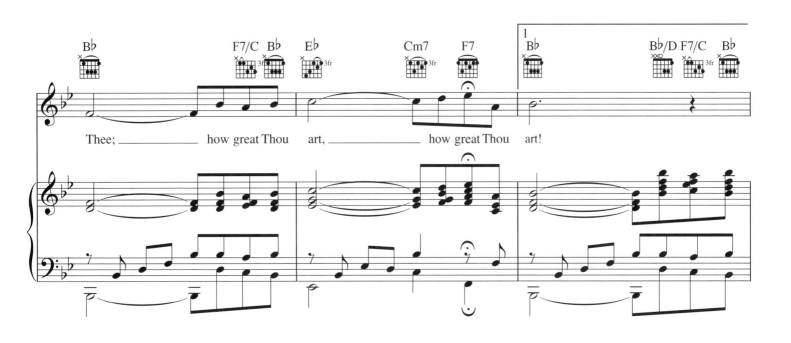

Thee; _____ how great Thou art, _____ how great Thou art!

And when I art! _____

SO HIGH

Adapted and Arranged by
ELVIS PRESLEY

AMAZING GRACE

Adapted and Arranged by
ELVIS PRESLEY

A - maz - ing grace, how sweet the
we've been there ten thou - sand

sound that saved a wretch like me!
years, bright shin - ing as the sun.

I once was lost, but now I'm
We've no less days to sing God's

CRYING IN THE CHAPEL

Words and Music by
ARTIE GLENN

Slowly, with expression

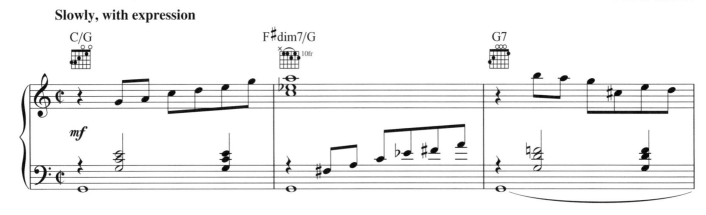

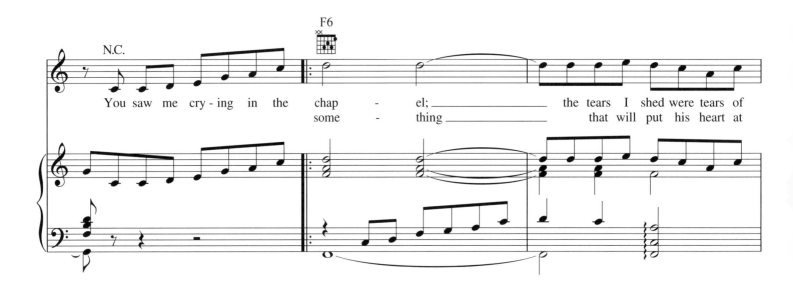

You saw me cry-ing in the chap - el; _____ the tears I shed were tears of
some - thing _____ that will put his heart at

joy. _____ I know the mean-ing of con - tent - ment, _____
ease. _____ There is on - ly one true an - swer: _____

YOU'LL NEVER WALK ALONE

from CAROUSEL

Lyrics by OSCAR HAMMERSTEIN II
Music by RICHARD RODGERS

With great warmth, like a hymn

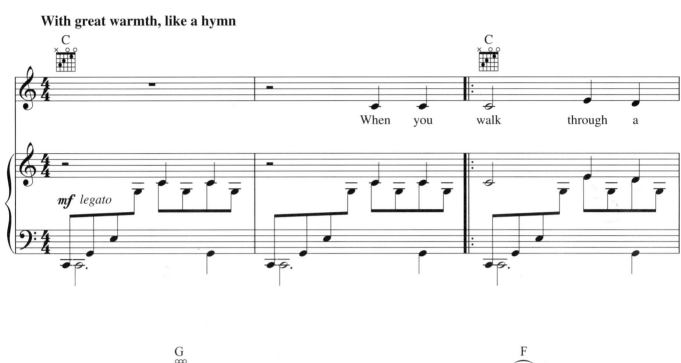

When you walk through a

storm, hold your head up high, and don't be a-

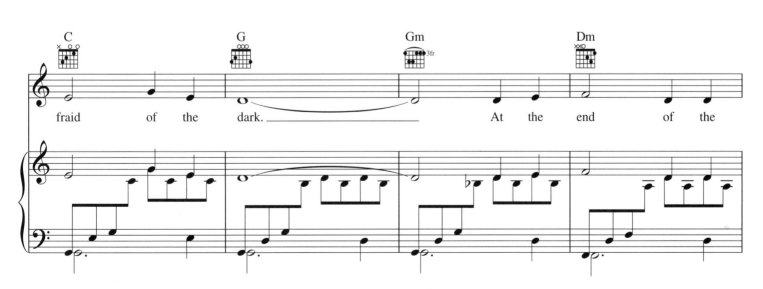

fraid of the dark. _____ At the end of the

on, with hope in your heart, and you'll nev - er

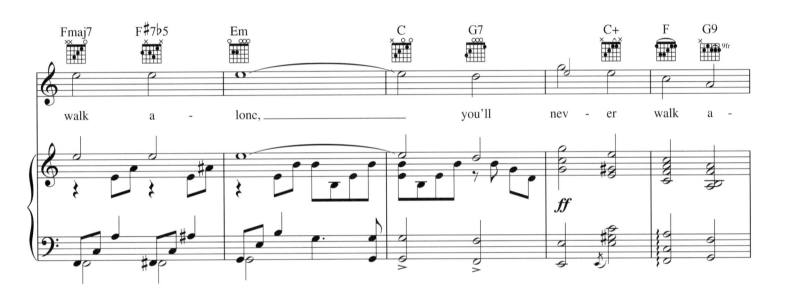

walk a - lonc, _____ you'll nev - er walk a -

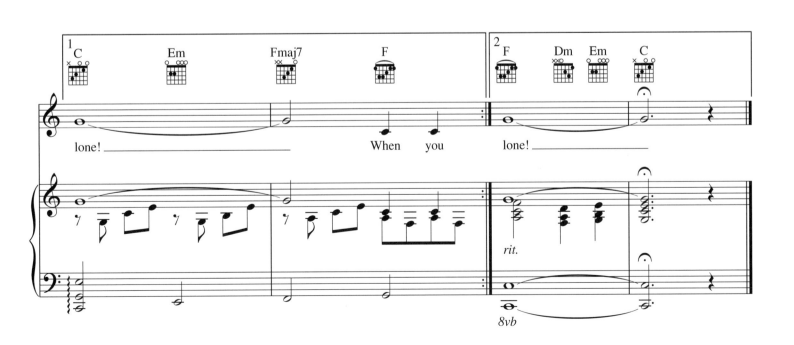

lone! _____ When you lone! _____

SWING DOWN, SWEET CHARIOT

Adapted and Arranged by
ELVIS PRESLEY

D.S. al Coda

just want - ed to see how a char - i - ot feel. _____ } Why don't you
Just want - ed to lay down his heav - y load. _____

CODA C7 F

oth - er side. Well, I got a

C7

Fa - ther in the Prom - ised Land, _____ ain't gon - na

F7

stop un - til I shake His hand. _____ Rock me, Lord,

IN MY FATHER'S HOUSE
(Are Many Mansions)

Words and Music by
ELVIS PRESLEY

In my Fa- ther's House are man - y man - sions. _____
died up - on the cross to bear my sor - row, _____

_____ If it were not true, He would have told me
free- ly died that souls like you might have new

so. He has gone a - way to
life. But I know that soon there'll

I BELIEVE IN THE MAN IN THE SKY

Words and Music by
RICHARD HOWARD

MILKY WHITE WAY

Arranged by
ELVIS PRESLEY

HIS HAND IN MINE

Words and Music by
MOSIE LISTER

WHERE COULD I GO

Words and Music by
JAMES B. COATS

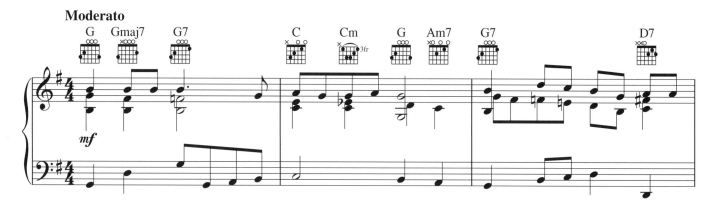

Liv - ing be - low in this old sin - ful world,
Neigh - bors are kind, I love them ev - 'ry one,
Life here is grand with friends I love so dear,

hard - ly a com - fort can af - ford; striv - ing a - lone to
we get a - long in sweet ac - cord; but when my soul needs
com - fort I get from God's own Word; yet when I face the

IF THE LORD WASN'T WALKING BY MY SIDE

Words and Music by
HENRY SLAUGHTER

Moderate Shuffle

RUN ON

Adapted and Arranged by
ELVIS PRESLEY

Well, you may run on ___ for a long time. ___ (Run on for a

long time.) ___ Run on ___ for a long time. ___ Let me

tell you God Al-might-y's gon-na cut you down. Go tell ___ that long-tongued

LEAD ME, GUIDE ME

Words and Music by
DORIS AKERS

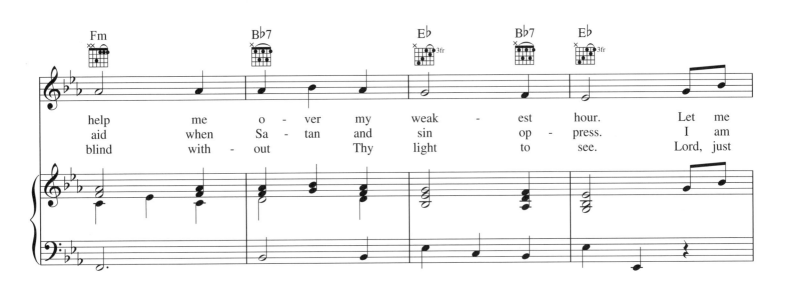

through the dark - ness Thy face to see;
put - ting all ____ my trust in Thee;
al - ways let me Thy ser - vant be;

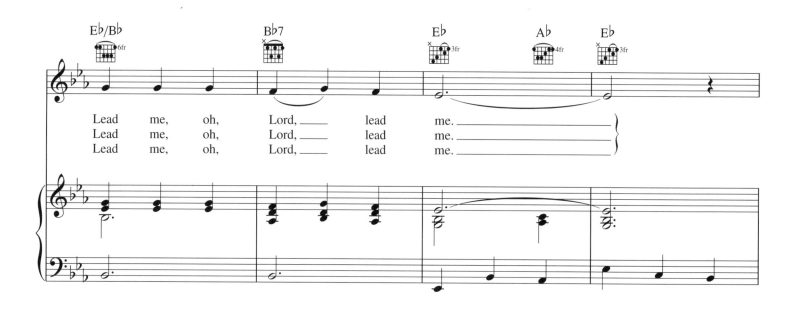

Lead me, oh, Lord, ____ lead me. ____
Lead me, oh, Lord, ____ lead me. ____
Lead me, oh, Lord, ____ lead me. ____

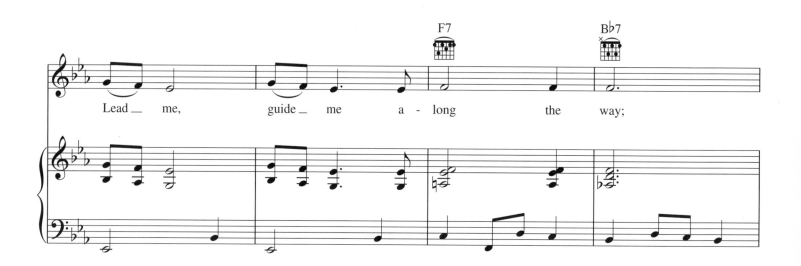

Lead __ me, guide __ me a - long the way;

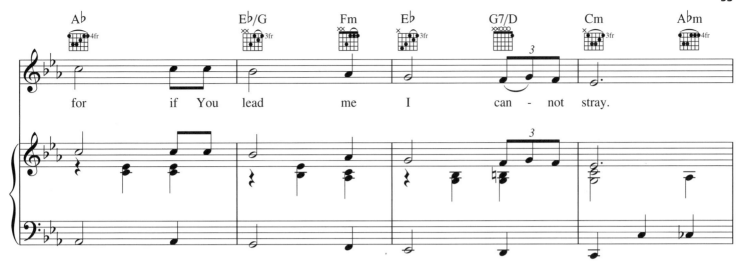

for if You lead me I can - not stray.

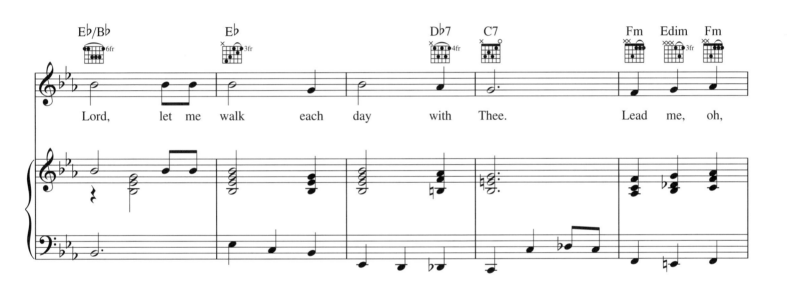

Lord, let me walk each day with Thee. Lead me, oh,

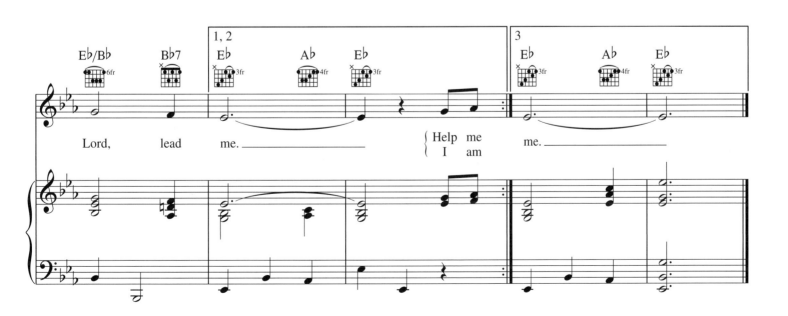

Lord, lead me. _____ Help me me. _____
I am

HE TOUCHED ME

Words and Music by
WILLIAM J. GAITHER

With an easy flow

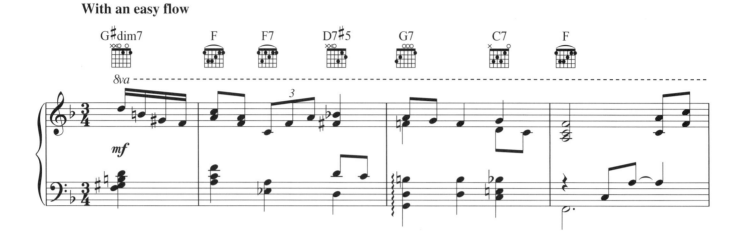

Shack - led by a heav - y bur - den ____
Since I met this bless - ed Sav - ior, ____

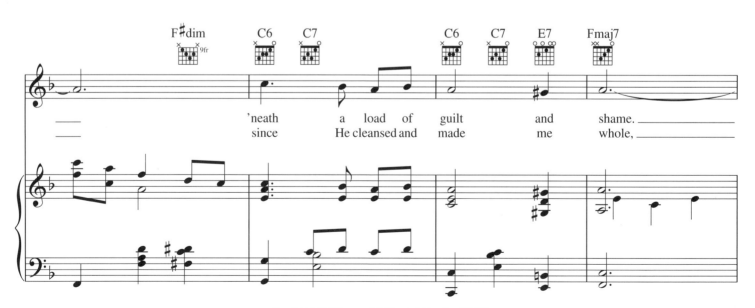

____ 'neath a load of guilt and shame. ____
____ since He cleansed and made me whole, ____

JOSHUA FIT THE BATTLE

Adapted and Arranged by
ELVIS PRESLEY

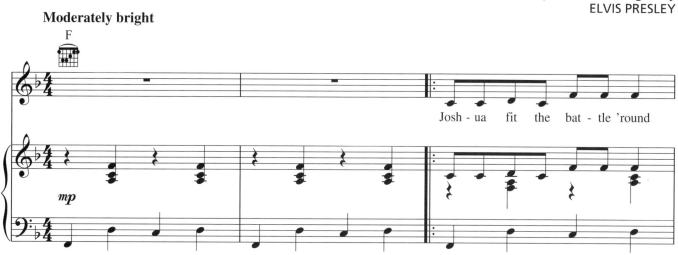

Josh - ua fit the bat - tle 'round

Jer - i - cho __ (a-round) Jer - i - cho __ (a-round) Jer - i - cho. __ Josh-ua fit the bat - tle of

Jer - i - cho __ and the walls come tum - bl - in' down. (God knows it.) down. 1. Good

Josh-ua fit the bat-tle 'round Jer - i - cho, _ (a - round) Jer - i - cho, _ (a - round) Jer - i - cho. _

Josh-ua fit the bat-tle of Jer - i - cho _ and the walls come tum-bl-in' down. down, down, down, down,
(God knows it.)

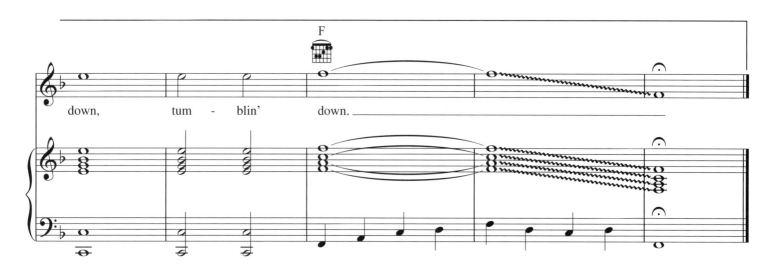

down, tum - blin' down. _____

Additional Lyrics

4. Up to the walls of Jericho,
   He marched with spear in hand;
   "'Go blow them ram horns," Joshua cried,
   "'Cause the battle is in my hand."

5. You may talk about your men of Gideon,
   You may talk about the King of Saul,
   Well, there's none like Joshua
   At the Battle of Jericho.

6. They tell me, great God, that Joshua's spear
   Was well nigh twelve feet long.
   And upon his hip was a double-edged sword
   And his mouth was a Gospel horn.

7. Yet bold and brave he stood,
   Salvation in his hand,
   "Go blow them ram horns," Joshua cried,
   "'Cause the devil can't do you no harm."

PRECIOUS LORD, TAKE MY HAND
(Take My Hand, Precious Lord)

Words and Music by
THOMAS A. DORSEY

Slow, with spirit

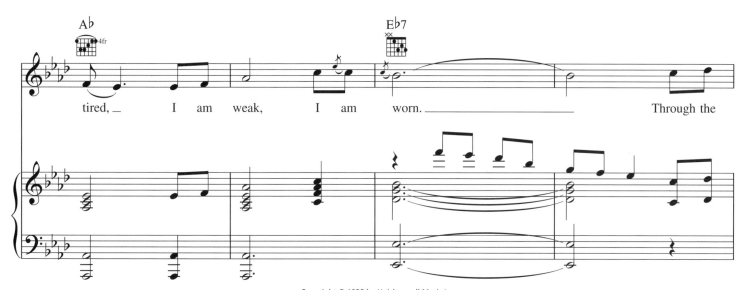

IF WE NEVER MEET AGAIN

Words and Music by
ALBERT E. BRUMLEY

REACH OUT TO JESUS

Words and Music by
RALPH CARMICHAEL

Is your bur-den heav-y _____ as you bear it all a-
lone? _____ Does the road you trav-el _____ har-bor

WHO AM I

Words and Music by
RUSTY GOODMAN

Moderately, not too slow

Lyrics:

When I think of how He
mind - ed of His

came, so far from Glo - ry, came and
words, "I'll leave thee nev - er. Just be

dwelt a - mong the low - ly such as
true, I'll give to you a life for -

HELP ME

Words and Music by
LARRY GATLIN

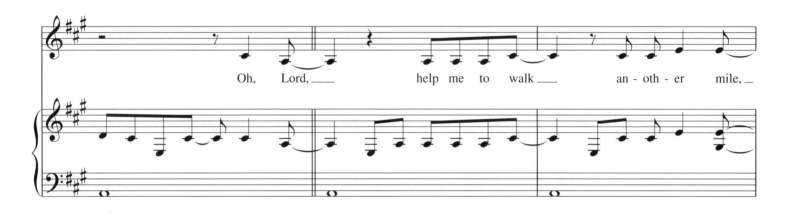

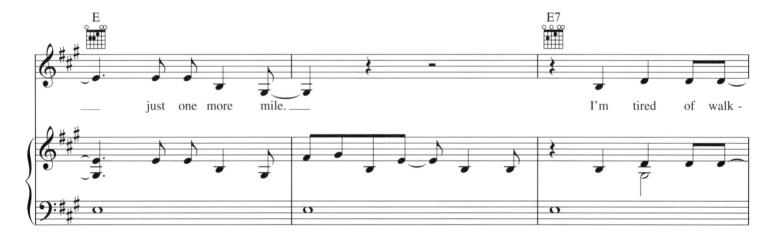

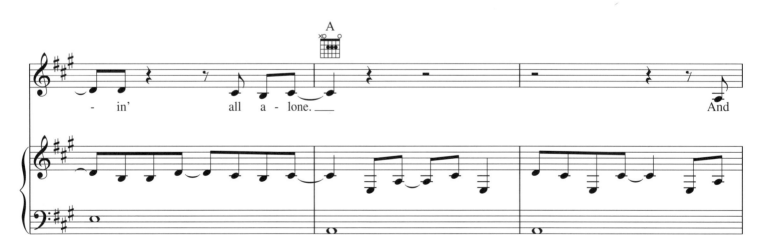

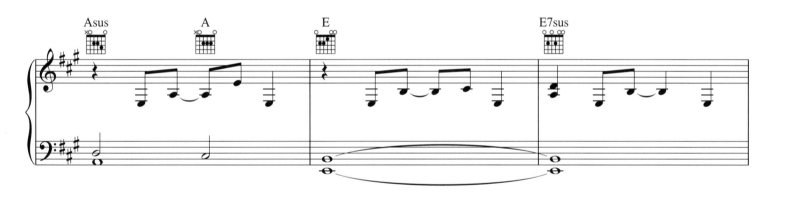

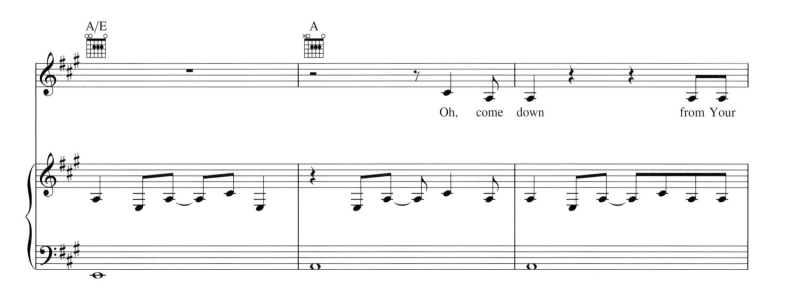

Oh, come down from Your

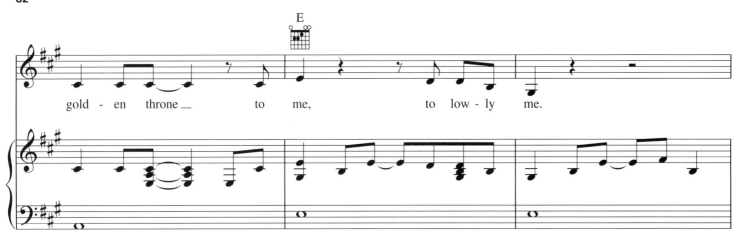

gold - en throne ___ to me, to low - ly me.

I need to feel the touch ___ of Your ten - der hand.

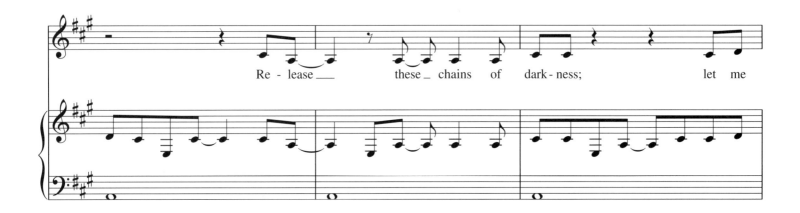

Re - lease ___ these ___ chains of dark - ness; let me

see, Lord, let me see just where I fit in - to ___

D.S. al Coda

AN EVENING PRAYER

By C.M. BATTERSBY
and CHAS. H. GABRIEL

(There'll Be)
PEACE IN THE VALLEY
(For Me)

Words and Music by
THOMAS A. DORSEY

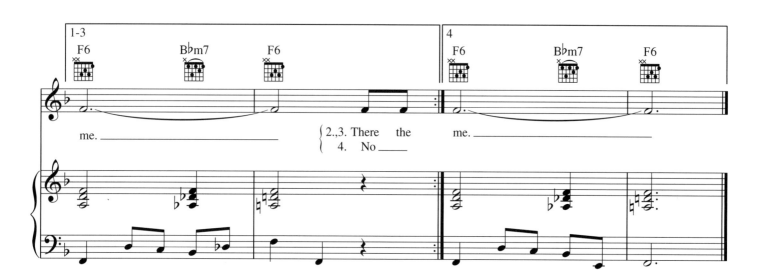

Additional Lyrics

4. No headaches or heartaches or misunderstands,
No, confusion or trouble won't be.
No frowns to defile, just a big endless smile,
There'll be peace and contentment for me.
Chorus

HAUNTED HOTELS

OF THE

WEST

by Bruce A. Raisch

This is a limited first edition.

THE
DONNING COMPANY
PUBLISHERS

Right: The Crescent Hotel in Eureka Springs, Arkansas.

Haunted Hotels

OF THE
West

by Bruce A. Raisch

The Donning Company Publishers
184 Business Park Drive, Suite 206
Virginia Beach, VA 23462

Steve Mull, General Manager
Barbara Buchanan, Office Manager
Anne Cordray, Editor
Jolene Blevins, Graphic Designer
Derek Eley, Imaging Artist
Tonya Hannink, Marketing Specialist
Pamela Engelhard, Marketing Advisor

Library of Congress Cataloging-in-Publication Data

Raisch, Bruce A., 1956-
  Haunted hotels of the West / by Bruce A. Raisch. -- 1st edition.
       p. cm.
  Includes bibliographical references.
  ISBN 978-1-57864-581-7
  1. Haunted hotels--West (U.S.) I. Title.
  BF1474.5.R35 2009
  133.1'22--dc22

                2009029311

Printed in the United States of America at Walsworth Publishing Company, Marceline, Missouri

Dedication

As always, my book is dedicated to a family member who is a U.S. military veteran. I gladly dedicate my fourth book to Donald Head. He served in the Air Force with my father. They met in 1956 and became life-long friends while on duty in North Africa during the Suez Crisis. This is also where and when I was born. At this point Don became more than a family friend; he became my Godfather. He has always been encouraging and supportive to me in my endeavors. While writing my first two books he took it upon himself to send me stacks of papers and books to help in the research. That's just the kind of person he is.

Donald Head served in the United States Air Force from 1955 to 1979.

Donald Head with his K-9 guard dog, Falko. This photo was taken in Tripoli, Libya. Notice the palm tree in the background.

Acknowledgments

First and foremost I would like to both acknowledge and thank the owners, management, and staff of all the hotels in this book. Personnel at these inns were always cheerful, helpful, and professional. If they weren't, the establishment was not put into the book. Also, the stories from cleaning crews, night auditors, and front desk clerks added greatly to this book. Frequently I was given personal tours and allowed to check out any and all structures from basement to attic.

I would like to thank Judy O'Leary for all the calls she made and the contacts she has provided me and for being such a great fan.

I would like to acknowledge John Thomas and the Supernatural Investigations. They were generous with their time and always willing to provide additional contacts and technical assistance. They were particularly helpful with my research on the Lemp

Out west, the environment can be tough on things, even businesses.

Mansion; a place they specialize in.

I would like to express gratitude to Jara Tyson, a friend who provided source material, contacts, and personal stories. She is originally from the Arcadia Valley in the northern Ozarks.

I would like to express my appreciation to Dr. Joseph Swope Sr. for answering technical questions and his help with medical history.

I would like to state my appreciation for Karen and Keith Bloodworth. The couple frequently joins me for a portion of my book research trips. Karen helps with photography and computer work. Keith just shows up, but he does it well.

I would like to give a mention to my publisher the Donning Company Publishers and its general manager Steve Mull. They have always been helpful and honest. In these days one must give notice when one's word over the phone, Internet, or a handshake is as good as a contract.

I would like to give a special thanks to my new secretary Dianne Haas. She worked tirelessly and without complaint. Her professional advice was much appreciated.

And last but not least, thanks to Patricia Cracchiola for helping with the final production.

Deep snow is why western hotels and saloons had two-story outhouses.

Contents

About the Book

I wrote most of this book while spending the winter in an old farmhouse deep in the Ozark woods. The house was seven-tenths of a mile down a dead end dirt road and came with a pack of coyotes for company. Often the pack gathered just outside my door and howled a serenade. The fireplace roared a reply. I played music, burned candles, and drank hot tea by the gallon. Just for the record, my teacup was a souvenir from the Stanley Hotel and had the word "RedЯum"in blood red lettering on its side.

I don't always stay in hotels. Sometimes the accommodations look like this.

This book is a collection of claims, legends, and stories of spirits at forty inns scattered across a dozen states of the Great American West. I tried to include all the alleged ghosts at these inns but space did not allow for all the ghost stories. Some places like the Crescent, Lemp, and Stanley could and have had whole books written about just them.

Included is a short history of each place and how it ties in with the alleged ghosts. Next, there is a section that discusses the location's services and things nearby to see and do. At the end of each is the inn's contact information and website. For your convenience these hotels are grouped into their own geographic regions. These regions and their hotels are all listed on pages 10 and 11. This book neither tries to prove, nor disprove, the existence of ghosts or that any hotels contained within this work are haunted. I did not examine these inns using any scientific equipment such as EMF (electro magnetic fluctuation) meters or thermal image devices. Investigations were conducted on an historical basis. The purpose of this book is to inform and entertain, and just maybe, help preserve part of this country's history.

Most of the information for this book was obtained by personally visiting each and every hotel listed. I interviewed owners, managers, desk clerks, cleaning crews, hotel guests, local paranormal groups, and others for information. For research purposes I ate, drank, slept, or took the scheduled tour at most of the hotels, and when possible, spent the night in one of the haunted rooms. Additional information was acquired from magazine or newspaper articles, the Internet, local and state historical societies,

8

chambers of commerce, local post offices, and more. Approximately a fourth of the hotels in this volume are ones I bumped into on my own and will not be found in other books.

I spent as little as one hour or as much as two days at these places. It is quite the interesting but sometimes creepy list of places. Five of the locations had been hospitals, two funeral homes, and one TB sanatorium in their past. On the interesting side, the vast majority of buildings in this book are on the National Register of Historic Places.

You learn a number of things while researching a book like this. For instance, not all hotels like to be called haunted. On the other hand other hotels market their ghosts into gold. You also notice some stories pop up again and again. I lost count of the number of places that claim a ghost named "The Lady in White." One possible explanation is that ghosts are frequently seen as spectral forms of glowing light that still allows one to still see features such as age or gender. A female ghost glowing in such a manner could easily get the nickname as "The Lady in White." Other possible explanations could be an urban legend or someone simply copying a good story.

The inns contained within this book vary greatly in size, services, style, and price. Some were so small they only had three guest rooms; others were large complexes of buildings spread out over acres of land. No one hotel is for everyone, but I enjoyed my visit to each one in this book. The one thing they did all have in common was that they were nice to all who walked through their doors. If they weren't, I just left them out of the book. I must admit that a few structures were showing their age in a couple of spots. Other locations, especially the high-end resorts, were a little pricy for some. I must also admit that some places seemed a lot less haunted than others—just telling it like it is.

One oddity, no matter how many stories the hotel had, they would omit numbering a floor the thirteenth. Also, quite often the first floor is on the second story. Hotels call the first story the main or lobby floor, then the second story is called the first floor and its rooms number as such, i.e., 101. The rest of the floors of the hotel follow this sequence. I call the second story the second floor. When I stayed at the Jerome Grand Hotel I was in Room 32 on the fourth floor. Often while doing research I wasn't really sure what actual floor the writer was referring to in their story. The mess is easy for you to work around, just ask at the front desk of the inn!

If you can't visit these places, just travel through this volume. I can't promise you a good night's sleep, but I think you'll enjoy the book. If you would like to provide additional information, make comments, ask questions, or order any of my other books, email me at: bar4916@yahoo.com. All photography, unless otherwise noted was done by the author. These books are made in the USA. They're actually printed in Marceline, Missouri, the boyhood home of Walt Disney.

9

List of Haunted Hotels

Big Sky Country

• **Chico Hot Springs Resort and Day Spa**
(Pray, Montana)

• **Fairweather Inn**
(Virginia City, Montana)

• **Grand Hotel**
(Big Timber, Montana)

• **Many Glacier Hotel**
(Glacier National Park, East Glacier, Montana)

• **Nevada City Hotel**
(Nevada City, Montana)

Black Hills

• **Hotel Alex Johnson**
(Rapid City, South Dakota)

• **The Bullock Hotel**
(Deadwood, South Dakota)

• **Franklin Hotel and Casino**
(Deadwood, South Dakota)

Great Plains

• **Argo Hotel**
(Crofton, Nebraska)

• **The Elms Resort and Spa**
(Excelsior Srpings, Missouri)

• **Hotel Savoy**
(Kansas City, Missouri)

• **Stone Lion Inn**
(Guthrie, Oklahoma)

• **The (Alonzo) Ward Plaza Hotel and Suites**
(Aberdeen, South Dakota)

Mississippi Valley

• **Lemp Mansion**
(St. Louis, Missouri)

• **Rockcliffe Mansion**
(Hannibal, Missouri)

Northern Rockies

• **Ben Lomond Suite Hotel**
(Ogden, Utah)

• **Brown Palace Hotel and Spa**
(Denver, Colorado)

• **Elk Mountain Hotel**
(Elk Mountain, Wyoming)

• **Jameson Inn**
(Wallace, Idaho)

• **Occidental Hotel**
(Buffalo, Wyoming)

- **Stanley Hotel**
(Estes Park, Colorado)

- **Virginian Hotel**
(Medicine Bow, Wyoming)

Ozarks

- **Arcadia Academy Bed and Breakfast**
(Arcadia, Missouri)

- **Crescent Hotel and Spa**
(Eureka Springs, Arkansas)

- **The Palor Bed and Breakfast**
(Ironton, Missouri)

Sage Brush Country

- **Enders Hotel**
(Soda Springs, Idaho)

- **Idaho City Hotel**
(Idaho City, Idaho)

- **Lava Hot Springs Inn**
(Lava Hot Springs, Idaho)

Southwest

- **Copper Queen Hotel**
(Bisbee, Arizona)

- **Gadsden Hotel**
(Douglas, Arizona)

- **Jerome Grand Hotel**
(Jerome, Arizona)

- **Plaza Hotel**
(Las Vegas, New Mexico)

- **St. James Hotel**
(Cimarron, New Mexico)

- **The Lodge**
(Cloudcroft, New Mexcio)

Yellowstone Territory

- **The Irma**
(Cody, Wyoming)

- **Lake Yellowstone Hotel**
(Yellowstone National Park, Wyoming)

- **Mammoth Hot Springs Hotel**
(Yellowstone National Park, Wyoming)

- **Old Faithful Inn**
(Yellowstone National Park, Wyoming)

- **Pollard Hotel**
(Red Lodge, Montana)

- **Togwotee Mountain Lodge**
(Moran, Wyoming)

Big Sky Country

Big Sky Country is the nickname for the great state of Montana. The phrase originated with the American Plains Indians who called it "The Land of the Big Sky." If you travel east to west in this beautiful and huge state, you soon realize why they gave this place such a name. Like the rest of the Great Plains, this is a wonderful place for star gazing and landscape photography. Majestic mountains dominate the western third of the state.

This state offers some of the best fly-fishing in the world as well as great opportunities for hiking and horseback riding. It contains Glacier National Park as well as the northern entrance to Yellowstone National Park. With its great size, astounding beauty, and wide variety of terrain, Montana offers a multiplicity of vacation opportunities. In other words, there's lots of ways to have fun there.

This section contains five allegedly haunted Montana inns. They are not the only hotels in the state that claim they are haunted, but they do represent a varied and interesting cross-section of the group.

Chico Hot Springs Resort and Day Spa

The Chico Hot Springs Lodge is a resort that many Hollywood celebrities love to visit and one that its first owners refuse to leave. The wife of the first owner was one Percie Knowles. She was a tough, stubborn, and independent frontier woman. She was the driving force that put this place on the map and now she is the most active of its two ghosts. She has been called both "The Lady in White" and "The Lonely Lady." She appears as a glowing apparition. She also has the impolite habit of staring at those who see her. Her favorite room to haunt is Room 346, where she spent her final years at the resort. She is most often seen on the third floor and usually during the winter. Her appearance is accompanied by the strong smell of flowers and intense cold. Guests, staff, and security have seen her.

Steven King could have used this ghost for inspiration. There are many stories from security and staff of noises coming from Room 346 while no guests are checked into it. When they go to investigate they are often greeted by a room empty of any person or any apparent source of noise. Other times the investigator is greeted by a blast of cold air and the sight of an empty rocking chair rocking back and forth on its own accord. Percie spent hours in this same rocker. If the staff moves the chair it just ends up back next to the window sooner or later. The hotel gets many requests to just see the room, although these same people frequently decline to spend the night in it.

One story or legend about Percie that has been widely told is that of her Bible.

The homey front entrance to the Chico Resort.

It was found in the attic on a small table with a wooden chair next to it. While the table, chair, and floor were thick with dust, the Bible was entirely free of it. The Bible lays open to the Psalms as if someone were reading it and had just put it down. Employees would turn the page to a different part of the Bible but upon their return the pages had been turned back. Other times a feather and a handkerchief had been placed on the Bible but again when the employee returned both items had disappeared leaving the Bible still open to the same page of the Psalms. Eventually the furniture was moved and the Bible placed in Percie's room.

There are a lot of "Percie" stories. One great source is *Big Sky Ghosts—Eerie True Tales of Montana, Volume II* by Debra D. Munn. It contains a number of scary stories including one that is well known in Montana. In the early pre-dawn hours one Sunday morning during May 1986, two security guards just couldn't believe their eyes, so they tried taking a picture. They were making their rounds and had just entered the lobby when one froze, pointed, and muttered, "Look."

Before their amazed eyes floated a white flimsy figure. Next to the piano, glowing like a light, it hovered above the floor while staring at them. You could clearly see the head and upper body but the rest was a smoky formless mass. This stare-down was supposed to have gone on for two minutes. That night must have seemed like an eternity for the two guards. One guard finally got the notion and courage to walk around the ghost and get a Polaroid camera from the office. He took a picture without a flash. When he did, the ghost faded away like smoke. Unfortunately the photo results were very poor and only showed a tiny white dot.

Most of the ghost spottings seem to be of Percie, although sometimes people claim to see a ghost that is male in appearance. He is seen wearing either a suit or a heavy overcoat, both of old period dress. He is

A sign at the entrance to the ghost town of Chico.

The pool is filled with water from the Chico Hot Springs.

always said to have a beard. He, like Percie, has the eerie habit of appearing as a floating apparition. The places he most frequently appears are the dining room, the saloon, and an employee area above the bar called the annex. Once he was spotted sitting with the apparition of Percie. Like Percie, he hovers, moves in a floating motion, and often hangs around for a good number of minutes. In a couple of chilling accounts he has approached those who have spotted him. His sightings are also accompanied by extreme cold. Many think this is the ghost of Bill Knowles, Percie's husband.

There are a lot of other strange stories here. They include piano music while no one is sitting at the piano, the late night sound of doors slamming on the third floor, feeling an unseen presence when working alone in a room, and in one case the moaning of a woman. A security guard tried for forty-five minutes to find the source of the sounds but failed. One more story is of candles lighting themselves in the kitchen. In fact, the kitchen seems to have even more activity than Room 346. Reports of cookware, dishes, and furniture falling, moving, and having been moved on their own are numerous. On my visit it was a story I heard repeatedly from the staff. Late night employees will hear noises from the kitchen after it's closed. When they investigate, they don't find a source of the noise or things such as chairs being moved around from their former places, etc. Percie and Bill have both been seen in the dining room and Percie in the kitchen. Reports of ghostly activities go back to 1967 and the owners before the current owners. They claim a number of paranormal experiences and blamed them on the Knowles even then. But not all blame it on the Knowles. With this much activity they say some of it may stem from the hotel's former hospital days.

Bill and Percie opened the hotel under the name Chico Warm Springs Hotel on June 20, 1900. Then, over Percie's objections, Bill expanded by adding a dance hall and saloon next to the hotel. This made the business an even bigger success. Still, Percie objected to alcohol on the property on moral grounds. Maybe Bill should have listened to her because on April 22, 1910, he died of cirrhosis of the liver. He was laid to rest in the nearby Chico cemetery. This left Percie to run the business and raise their twelve-year-old son, Radbourne. The first thing Percie did after burying her husband was to close the hotel's saloon. The hotel had already been advertised for the therapeutic effects of its hot springs, but now Percie turned it into an all out healthcare resort. In 1912 she convinced the renowned Dr. George A. Townsend to set up office in the hotel. This brought the resort credibility and even a degree of fame. Next she added a hospital wing to the hotel and enlarged its hot pools. Dr. Townsend worked at Chico Hot Springs for the next thirteen years until his retirement in 1925. Even though other doctors were brought in to replace him, the hospital never again enjoyed its high reputation and business declined. The Great Depression brought a further decline in business. Another blow to both Percie and the business happened when Radbourne

left to get married. By this point both Percie and the resort went into a serious physical decline. Eventually the emotional and physical strain was too much and Percie suffered a mental breakdown. She spent more and more time in Room 346, rocking in her chair and staring out the window. Finally, in 1936 she was committed to the state hospital in Warm Springs, Montana. She died there four and a half years later. Radbourne died in 1943, and after his passing the resort went through a series of owners. Then in 1973, Mike and Eve Art purchased the property.

The hotel complex was changed from a health resort to a fun and relaxing vacation getaway destination. The Arts thoroughly refurbished the place and added a number of improvements. The resort became a favorite rest stop for numerous Hollywood stars. Many of their photos, along with numerous historical black and whites, adorn the walls of the main lodge. Some of the stars arrived by private plane, landing on a grass strip next to the hotel. Today it is once again a thriving business. Percie would be proud. Maybe that's why she still hangs around.

Cabins and a complex of other buildings surround the main lodge. There is an outdoor pool and its waters are fed by the hot springs. The resort has an award-winning restaurant, a complete day spa, an espresso bar with a gift shop and, over Percie's objection, a saloon. For informal dining there is the Poolside Grille. The grounds include several gardens, a greenhouse, a hiking trail, and a shooting range. They offer a wide variety of accommodations from A-Frame chalets to suites. Some of the cabins even have Jacuzzis. I found the staff to be cheerful, helpful, and professional. Their brochures also claim they invented dog friendly, for those traveling with the family pooch. Available nearby is horseback riding and whitewater rafting outfits. Also close at hand are the Yellowstone River and the ghost town of Chico. Yellowstone National Park is only thirty minutes to the south.

Contact Information
Highway 89 South
P.O. Box 29
Pray, MT 59065
406-333-4933
www.chicohotsprings.com

17

Fairweather Inn

Squeezed in tightly amongst a row of weather-beaten, false-fronted, wooden buildings on Virginia City's main business street, sits the small, two-story Fairweather Inn. This inn is very small, but not so small that a bowling alley couldn't fit on the building's lot. In fact a bowling alley and saloon used to occupy the site. It is claimed that people who stay in Room 10 can still sometimes hear the noises of the bowling lanes. The room is said to be haunted and the hotel and room have been the subject of a PBS episode. Much of the town and its multiple cemeteries are also said to be haunted. This includes a second haunted hotel, the Bonanza Inn.

The town itself can easily serve as an outdoor western museum and that alone is worth the visit. Bill Fairweather discovered gold here in Alder Creek during May 1863 and almost overnight the boomtown of Virginia City sprang up. At its peak there were over ten thousand people in this and the surrounding towns. Virginia City served as the area's main business, social, and transportation center until the early 1900s. One town, Nevada City, lies just a mile to the west and was a major competitor for business. Today it is still there and now competes with Virginia City for summer tourists. An excursion steam train connects the two towns and makes for a nice family outing. Back in Virginia City you have a number of restaurants, gift shops, antique stores, an old-time photo

The Fairweather Inn.

gallery, Old West saloon, a variety of lodging including bed and breakfasts, plus the Brewery Follies. Its building, Montana's first brewery, is now a live theater. Variety shows done in a cabaret style are put on twice daily. The town has a fine history museum that is packed with information about the area's past. There are a couple of old western cemeteries here, including a boot hill, and they are also alleged to be haunted by restless spirits.

The Fairweather Inn is owned by the State of Montana and leased to its current operators. Structures were built, rebuilt, and remodeled on this plot of land numerous times. It started in 1863 as a restaurant in a simple log structure. In 1866 the building was sold, probably enlarged and converted into a meat market. In the 1880s it was converted into a combination of a hotel, restaurant, and saloon. Frank McKeen bought it in

A fun way to tour the town.

1896. The building went through another major reconstruction. This included using materials from another hotel that had stood in Bannack, Montana. At this time its name was changed to the Anaconda Hotel, which operated with a bar and dining room. It was sold in 1935 to the Humphrey Gold Corporation and converted into a company office and

The tour train that runs between Nevada City and Virginia City.

dormitory. In 1946 Charles and Sue Bovey bought the property; and you guessed it—they remodeled the building. They reopened the hotel in 1946 even though they hadn't finished their remodeling. Its new name, the Fairweather Inn, was in honor of Bill Fairweather.

Located in the heart of town, the inn has fifteen rooms to rent. It is a two-story frame structure renovated in a blend of Victorian and western décor and furnished with antiques from the period. Five rooms have private baths and air conditioning. The rest have ceiling fans and shared baths.

Contact Information
301 West Wallace
P.O. Box 205
Virginia City, MT 59755
406-843-5377
www.aldergulchaccommodations.com

Grand Hotel

Nestled peacefully in the center of downtown Big Timber, Montana, is the Grand Hotel. Don't let the names fool you; both are quite cozy in size. In addition to being cozy the hotel is something else—haunted. There are supposed to be three ghosts here. One is the spirit of a Chinese laundry woman. In its early history, the Grand Hotel had a laundry in back that was mostly staffed with Chinese immigrants. The spirit is said to be one of these workers who died at the hotel. Her apparition has been seen by staff in the basement and the kitchen.

A second apparition is that of an older Caucasian woman. She has been seen by both guests and staff in Room 11. It is thought she was once a guest in that room.

The third ghost, also been seen by guests and staff, was described as "cute." She is a little girl with curly blond hair and a balloon or giant lollipop. She is spotted in the lobby and in the restaurants. One unknowing waitress once saw the little girl sitting at a dining table with a couple. The waitress assumed they were family. When taking their order she asked, "And what will the little girl have?" The couple replied, "What little girl?" When the waitress turned her head and hand to point at the girl, she was gone. The Grand was built in 1896 and has been fully restored to its original elegance. The interior was completely redone in the 1980s. Today the building is listed in the National Register of Historic Places.

The rooms are grandly furnished with Victorian era pieces. Some do not come with a bath. Their prices were quite reasonable and breakfast is included with the rooms. There are two separate dining rooms. One offers fine gourmet dining

The Grand Hotel.

The sign does say spirits.

with a nice wine selection. The other is the 1890 saloon. It offers casual dining in a room that has been completely restored to its nineteenth-century grandeur.

Nearby are two blue ribbon trout streams, the Boulder River and the Yellowstone River. Also nearby are the Gallatin National Forest and the Absaroka Mountains.

Contact Information
139 McLeod Street
P.O. Box 1242
Big Timber, MT 59011
406-932-4459
www.thegrand-hotel.com

Many Glacier Hotel

Resting on the shores of an alpine mountain lake all the while being surrounded on three sides by towering peaks is the Many Glacier Hotel. It would be difficult to find a hotel with a more beautiful setting. In addition to the beautiful setting this alpine inn is rumored to come with a restless spirit or two.

Many Glacier Hotel.

The majority of the hauntings are said to occur on the third and fourth floors of the south annex. There are claims of doors slamming and of disembodied footsteps. Interviews with some staff mention the usual feeling of being watched but also for a good while the clock in Room 416 kept running backwards. No explanation was ever found.

The best stories came from the head bellman. His tales reminded me of the movie, *The Shining*. They were stories he had gotten from the winter caretaker, who worked alone at the inn during the off-season. The caretaker's first major experience with a possible ghost involved his thermos. The winters are brutal and the caretaker liked his hot coffee. One day when he decided it was coffee break time but found the thermos wasn't where he remembered leaving it. He spent hours searching for it, but no luck and no hot coffee. Then one afternoon, weeks later, he was at his desk doing some paperwork and when he glanced up, there was his thermos. He picked it up and could feel that it was still full. He must have thought he was losing his mind. When he opened it, the coffee was still hot! He almost quit that night.

The second story concerned the liquor cabinet. The establishment serves alcohol. In the winter all the liquor is locked up in a glass cabinet. One day the lone caretaker was checking out the south annex. Just as he came to the landing on the third floor he saw there were two unopened bottles of wine. He recognized the wine as some the hotel carried. He went back to the main building and checked out the liquor cabinet. Sure enough, it had been opened and two bottles were missing. The caretaker noticed something else. Whoever had unlocked the liquor cabinet and placed the two bottles in the third-floor hallway had managed to do so without leaving

The Red Jammer bus.

boating on the lake, be aware that the water is beyond cold, it is often around 38° or colder. If you fall in and aren't close to shore, death could be just minutes away. Shock or hypothermia can incapacitate a victim in seconds. If you avoid shock or drowning, death by hypothermia can occur in only minutes. One tip, no matter what month you go, pack some warm clothing. The weather can easily turn cold here, even on an August day.

The hotel has a restaurant and a large inviting fireplace in the lobby. There are free hotel tours and evening naturalist programs. There is a boat dock in front of the lodge on Swiftcurrent Lake. Boat rentals are available. Activities include boating, fishing, hiking, horseback riding, and my favorite, the "Red Jammer" tour buses. These beautiful and historic vehicles take you to Logan Pass via the eastern portion of the Going to the Sun Road. This famous highway is an engineering marvel and one of the most scenic drives in the world.

any footprints in the snow. The only ones the caretaker could find were his own.

Construction of the Many Glacier Hotel started in 1914, and the first guests were able to check in on July 4th of the next year. The southern annex was completed two years later.

A couple of cautions here—if you go for a hike remember this is grizzly bear territory. Also grizzlies are not the only dangerous animals here. These are wild animals. They are not part of a petting zoo, so keep your distance. If you go

Contact Information

P.O. Box 147
East Glacier, MT 59434
406-732-4411
www.glacierparkinc.com

The South Annex.

Wildlife will come right up to the building.

Nevada City Hotel

Right next to the entrance of the Old West tourist town of Nevada City, Montana, stands the Nevada City Hotel. Nearby is a mining museum. Across the street (the only street) is an outdoor railroad museum. Just beyond you can see the massive piles of tailings left behind by the mining dredge. The site of Nevada City is frequently used as a movie set and local residents have been hired as film extras at one time or another. On my research trips there, I've always been entertained with a couple of their stories that just come up during conversations. In more ways than one, this is an extremely unique place.

The Nevada City Hotel.

The inn is surrounded by history. It is also occupied by a ghost. What's even better, this ghost made it into a movie, *Enemy of the People.*

The movie company was shooting a scene in the hotel lobby. The building had been cleared of all people prior to the filming to assure there was "all quiet on the set," despite that someone could be heard walking about Room 7 while the film was rolling; the sound was loud and distinct. You could also hear the sound of a chair being moved as if someone was adjusting its location so they could sit in it. When film crewmembers got to the room, the door was closed. Upon opening it they found no one in the room or even on the second floor. But a chair appeared to have been pulled away slightly from the room table as if someone had been sitting in it. I was told the noises were recorded and left in the film.

Still it is Room 9 on the second floor that is alleged to be the most haunted. Guests report strange and unexplainable noises. They also get the feeling that somebody or something else is in the room with them.

Next-door is the Star Bakery. Here you can get great food served with a side order of movie story. I once had blueberry cheesecake malt there and protested that it should have been labeled "potentially addictive."

On the other side of the hotel is the entrance to the Old West tourist town portion of Nevada

City. This is where you find the collection of historical buildings saved by the Boveys. It had been laid out to resemble a town of the Old West and comes complete with re-enactors. The buildings are furnished in an original manner and are full of normal everyday articles such as dishes, etc. The re-enactors wear period clothing and go about as they would have in the 1870s. When I was there some of the re-enactors were cooking and giving out free samples of frontier cuisine.

Just down the road from Nevada City is the competing tourist town of Virginia City and its two haunted hotels. These two towns are connected by an excursion steam train ride. There had previously been a Nevada City Hotel but it had burned down long ago. Then in the 1940s Charles and Sue Bovey, to preserve western history, started collecting old historic buildings from Montana, Wyoming, and Idaho and placing them in Nevada City. Using portions from some of these buildings they built another Nevada City Hotel on the site of the first one and opened it in 1959.

The front portion of the hotel was reconstructed from a 1860s stagecoach station. The station building was from a location south of Twin Bridges, Montana, and last known as Salisbury Station. The rear portion of the hotel was originally an employee dormitory at Canyon Hotel in Yellowstone National Park. The two-story outhouse attached to the hotel came from a large Montana residence. The hotel is a two-story wood structure. It has seventeen rooms to rent and a quaint lobby.

Contact Information
307 West Wallace
Virginia City, MT 59755
406-843-5377 • 800-829-2969, ext 4
host@aldergulchaccommodations.com
www.aldergulchaccommodations.com

Nevada City is proud of its film history.

The hotel has other facilities, in addition to this two-story outhouse.

28

Black Hills

Sitting darkly in the middle of the Great Plains is a mountain oasis known as the Black Hills. It is situated in southwest South Dakota with about a tenth of the area overlapping into northeast Wyoming. This Wyoming portion is where you will find Devils Tower. The reason why it's called the Black Hills is when seen from a far distance, the Ponderosa Pines that cover these mountains appear black. Its dramatic beauty has attracted movie directors from Alfred Hitchcock making *North by Northwest* to Kevin Costner and his *Dances with Wolves*. It is an outdoor paradise and high up on this country's list of national treasures. For good reason much has been written about the Black Hills including a book I have written about the area named, *Ghost Towns and Other Historical Sites of the Black Hills.*

There is much to see and do. A short list would have to include Mount Rushmore, Sturgis, Spearfish Canyon, Jewel Cave, and Wind Cave National Park. The Badlands are right next-door. Custer State Park, near Mount Rushmore, is the second largest state park in the country. Also for a fun step back into time, enjoy a steam train ride on the 1880 Railroad.

There are also at least three haunted hotels in these hills. Two of these inns are in the historic town of Deadwood. The cemetery is full of historic graves and is also allegedly haunted. A tour is given of the town's haunted places. All of this sort of puts the "Dead" into Deadwood. The third haunted hotel is in Rapid City, South Dakota.

Hotel Alex Johnson

Sitting as it does in downtown Rapid City, the Hotel Alex Johnson has an excellent location. It also has a gift shop, nightclub, restaurant, ballroom, its own small museum, oh yeah, and a couple of ghosts.

The ghosts here have caused a little bit of a stir. They have made the hotel a story on radio, TV, and in books and newspapers. The management even keeps a scrapbook about its hauntings behind the check-in counter in the lobby. The spirits have caused employees to quit suddenly, refuse the night shift, and not work on certain floors, especially the eighth.

The most thought provoking of the spirits would have to be "The Lady in White." Both staff and guests have seen her apparition. It is said she wanders the halls in a white gown, especially on the eighth floor. It is believed the spirit is that of a woman who checked into Room 812 and then, due to despair, leaped to her death. The newspaper, the *Rapid City Weekly News*, did report that a woman fell to her death from that room during the 1970s.

From there the story diverges into at least three separate versions. The one I relate here is the one the hotel provided. It was the woman's wedding day, which would explain the white dress. She fell into a state of deep despair after catching the groom with another woman that same day. Then in her depression, committed suicide by leaping from the window of their bridal suite. It is claimed that she moves objects, makes scary

When you step through the door of the Alex Johnson, you step back into time.

30

crying noises, and sometimes opens the window in Room 812.

There is a lot of phenomenon said to occur without any particularly known spirit to be associated with it. A poltergeist plagues the top floor of the hotel. The area is only used for storage now. When staff enters the floor, the furniture left there has been moved about and the lights turn themselves on and off. It is claimed one employee had a chair thrown down at him from the top-floor doorway while he was in the stairwell. This area is closed to the public.

There were a good number of claims I read in other sources that the staff confirmed for me as still occurring. One is that the elevator sometimes stops on the third floor for no apparent reason. In fact one desk clerk told of seeing the elevator take off from the lobby on its own and go to and stop on the third floor as if it were being operated by unseen hands. The elevator is inspected regularly and nothing has ever been found to explain this.

Visitors and staff have both reported hearing piano music coming from the ballroom. When they enter the ballroom there is no one at the piano or even in the room. The piano music isn't always confined to the ballroom but has been heard over the rest of the hotel at one time or another.

The Alex Johnson is easy to find in downtown Rapid City.

Besides the Lady in White, two other apparitions have been reported. The most frequently sighted one is that of an older gentleman. Hotel workers, guests, and especially the night security guards have seen him. This is thought to be the spirit of Alex Johnson. Some of the staff blame the unexplained elevator movements on him and even call out to let him know when they've had enough. They say it seems to work and the elevator hijacks will stop for the night.

The last visible spirit is that of a maid. A housekeeper complained that she had been frightened by a lady ghost watching her work. She said she was strangely dressed. While looking at old pictures of the hotel she noticed the maid's uniform from the late 1920s was the same strange clothing she noticed her staring ghost was wearing. She is now convinced she was being watched by a former maid of the hotel.

Some of the laughter and giggling that is heard comes from the spirit of a little girl. Her name was Brittney. She was a daughter of one of the cleaning ladies. One cleaning lady used to leave candy for Brittany in one of the rooms. When she would return the candy would be gone.

It is a handsome hotel. Its décor is an odd, yet attractive mixture of American Indian and German Tudor. The lobby has its own small history museum. Construction started on the hotel on August 19, 1927. The hotel had its grand opening on July 1, 1928. In 1958 director Alfred Hitchcock, actress Eva Marie Saint, and actor Cary Grant stayed at the hotel while filming the academy award-winning *North by Northwest*. Kevin Costner stayed here while filming *Dances with Wolves*. Numerous other Hollywood celebrities and at least six presidents have stayed here. The building is on the National Register of Historic Places. Over the years, the hotel has gone through numerous renovations and ownership changes. The last renovation in 1992 was a top to bottom affair. The top floor is still closed to the public. It had been an observatory, a penthouse, and the location of Rapid City's first radio station. Today it is used to store furniture and ghosts.

Contact Information
523 Sixth Street
Rapid City, SD 57701-2725
605-342-1210 • 800-888-ALEX (2539)
www.alexjohnson.com

The Bullock Hotel

They say the Bullock Hotel is haunted by a restless spirit but don't worry, they also claim the spirit is that of the town's first sheriff, Seth Bullock. It was said, and photos taken at the time back this up, that Seth could stare down a buffalo. Just his icy gaze was enough to make a noisy miner or rowdy bar patron back down. People at the Bullock today say he still has the same cold stare.

Seth Bullock was a leading citizen and businessman of Deadwood, and also was the founder and owner of the Bullock Hotel. Seth Bullock loved his hotel and ran a tight operation. He died of cancer during 1919 in Room 211. He was buried in the historic and allegedly haunted Mt. Moriah Cemetery with his fellow Deadwood citizens, Wild Bill Hickok and Calamity Jane.

It is claimed that Seth still roams the halls of his beloved hotel today. In fact more than just the halls, it seems old Seth has been spotted just about everywhere in the place. Of course his favorite place is Room 211 and the second most active area would be the basement, which is now a saloon, Seth's Cellar. People have claimed to have seen him on more than three dozen occasions.

He is often seen literally roaming the halls. When shown his photo, people claim that is the man they have seen. One story said Seth was even seen sitting outside the hotel. One morning during the summer of 2006 two ladies walking down the street turned and entered into the Bullock. On the way in one lady noticed a handsome dark–haired man in western apparel, sitting outside on a bench. She thought his appearance so remarkable that she guessed he might be a re-enactor or maybe even a real cowboy and said so to the other lady. Her friend replied, "What man?" With that they immediately turned around and went back outside but the man, or spirit, was gone in a matter of seconds. Later that weekend the lady who had spotted the cowboy bought a book as a trip souvenir.

The Bullock Hotel.

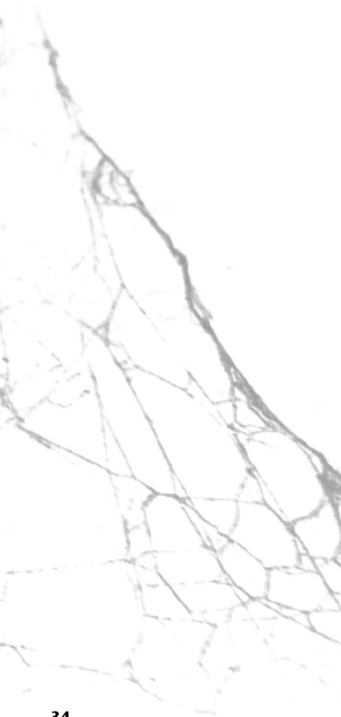

It was a history book of South Dakota and while leafing through it she made a shocking discovery. It had a photo that she swore was the exact likeness of the man she saw sitting in front of the Bullock. The photo caption said the man was Seth Bullock.

My favorite "Seth" story involves a lost little boy. A couple of grandparents and their seven-year-old grandson had checked into Room 306. The little boy left the room to find a vending machine. Soon the kid got turned around in the building and became lost. After a little while the grandfather became worried and decided to go look for the wayward little boy. He didn't have to look far; as soon as he opened his room door he saw the boy. He was standing there and just about to open the door himself. He explained that he had taken so long because he had become lost in the hotel, but a nice gentleman helped him find his way back. The next day when they were checking out, the little boy pointed to a picture of Mr. Bullock and said that he was the nice man that had helped him find his way back to his room. Besides Seth, some sources claim an

additional thirty-six spirits haunt this hotel. Whatever the number of ghosts, the Bullock appears to be a very spooky place.

It is claimed that phantom footsteps have been heard walking on all floors of the hotel. Showers seemingly turn themselves on. Lights and appliances turn themselves on and off. Radios have been known to turn from whatever station they're on to a country station instead, including when unplugged. Guess we know what music Seth prefers. Guests report hearing the weeping of a woman and other times the crying of a child. Whether footsteps or crying, when people poke their heads out of their rooms to investigate, they usually only find an empty hall, but occasionally they are greeted by a vanishing apparition. Orbs have been caught on film with everything from Polariods to video cams. In addition to orbs, various auroes, fuzzy lights, haze-like fog, and other phenomenon have been captured on film. The best places to catch something on film are Room 211 and Seth's Cellar bar room. Seth is not the only apparition that has been seen here. There is also the spirit of a little girl. She is usually spotted in the basement. This was one place small children were kept during typhoid fever and small pox outbreaks in Deadwood.

Either this place is very haunted or the staff is well trained in making up ghost stories. Every book, TV show, and website that mentions the Bullock has a collection of ghost stories that were personal experiences of the staff. I had no problem finding a number of employees that claimed to have had multiple unexplained experiences. There are dozens of stories about cleaning carts being moved when no one is looking, of bar stools spinning or being pushed by an unseen hand, and plates and glasses moving, falling off tables, or flying through the air on their own. Some reported hearing the piano mysteriously playing ragtime tunes on its own.

Downtown Deadwood.

Besides the activity in Seth's Cellar, the kitchen on the first floor and much of the second and third floors are also reported to be active. There are a total of eight guest rooms with a large number of reported paranormal experiences. These rooms are 205, 207, 209, 211, 302, 305, 313, and 314.

This hotel simply revels in its ghostly immortality. They advertise it in their hotel brochure. They give paid ghost tours. Their website is full of ghostly stories and photos. The staff keeps a scrapbook full of photos and guest ghost stories behind the check-in desk. In fact, customers frequently request a

35

haunted room. During my tour of the hotel a group was requesting haunted rooms and ghost tour information.

Fire was an early curse of the town of Deadwood. Often it roared through the streets destroying all in its path. In 1894 one of these fires burned down the Deadwood Hardware Store, and Seth bought the land that sat beneath its ashes. His intent was to go into the hotel business. In 1896, after two years of construction, his new hotel opened with a gala celebration.

It was completed with sixty rooms in a three-story brick structure. The hotel had all the modern conveniences and was considered fireproof.

The hotel was rebuilt in 1990. At that time the number of rooms were cut from over sixty to just twenty-eight. This allowed management to greatly enlarge the remaining rooms. The hotel does have suites. Numerous old photographs and other historical displays adorn the walls. A great deal of the first floor is now taken up by slot machines. There is also a gift shop, a bar,

and Bullys Restaurant on the main floor. The fine food, drinks, and stories of Seth's Cellar are just below. The building is a National Historic Registered Landmark and is well located in downtown Deadwood.

Contact Information
633 Main Street
Deadwood, SD 57732-1123
605-578-1745
Reservations: 800-336-1879
www.deadwood.org

Franklin Hotel and Casino

The Franklin Hotel is one of the haunted inns I located just by asking around. When asking questions in Deadwood more than one resident mentioned the Franklin Hotel. It is not something the hotel website mentions nor does management promote it to tourists but when I inquired at the front desk if anyone knew any stories about the place being haunted, the reply came back, "Yes." I didn't find any of the staff that had any personal experiences but a number of them did say that guests would often come to the front desk with stories of the unexplained. Televisions turn on or off by themselves. A lady in early period dress roams the halls on fourth floor, but it's the third floor that seems to generate the most stories of unusual experiences.

The staff was very friendly and helpful. They gave me a complete tour of the building. This included the basement and what they call "the Brain Room." The story is there was a maintenance man who suspected his wife was having an affair. So he obtained a shotgun, took it to work, and committed suicide in the hotel basement. He had leaned against a wooden support beam and turned the shotgun to his head. The blast pattern from numerous shotgun pellets is still plainly visible.

The Franklin Hotel.

After all of that, it turned out that his wife wasn't having an affair after all. One investigative note, there was no bloodstain visible on the wood beam.

After the tour they let me roam the hotel on my own.

I discovered in my interviews that the ghost seems to only bother the guests! I talked to the cleaning crew, maintenance personnel, managers, front desk people, and more. None had any experiences themselves but all had guests approach them with claims, stories, and/or questions about strange happenings.

The Franklin is located in the heart of historic Deadwood, South Dakota. Its grand opening was on June 4, 1903. It was constructed in the Greek revival style. The hotel was outfitted in an advanced manner for the time. The rooms featured electricity, phones, radiant heat, and running water.

Famous and historic guests that have stayed here include President Theodore Roosevelt, Babe Ruth, John Wayne, Pearl Buck, Gayle Sayers, and Kevin Costner.

Starting in the early 1990s the hotel owners began a major renovation of the building. The whole structure is being rebuilt from the ground up. The project is ongoing. The newly rebuilt first floor has the lobby, the Silverado Casino, a restaurant, a hair salon, a ladies spa, and two bars—one with live music.

Contact Information
700 Main Street
Deadwood, SD 57732
605-578-3670 • 800-688-1876
www.deadwood.org

The site of the alleged suicide.

Great Plains

A vast area of unbroken horizons awaits the adventurous traveler of the American West. Once called the Great American Desert, it is now known as the Great Plains. This is where the railroad met the buffalo and the plow met the prairie. It is a place of great beauty and great distances. It is a land of constant wind and of violent thunderstorms but of little or no shelter. Picnics can be a challenge. This is a place where many miles between towns and services are common. The phrase "just around the corner" has a whole different meaning here. Life can be hard on the prairie but its people have adapted and overcome the challenge. In short, it is an area with its own history, weather, culture, and way of life. It is not plain; it is unique.

The stars here have to be seen to be believed. With less air and light pollution the stars are brighter and clearer. One night I will never forget was spent under those stars. I had set up camp at some pullover off an isolated two-lane highway. It was so isolated no vehicle passed my campsite for a period of over ten hours! Since I pack my own firewood I was able to build a fire. Then I found a good radio station. The stars were so bright and looked so close it made me feel like I could reach up and pick one as if it were bright, ripe fruit from a tree. It was a wonderful way to spend an evening.

The Great Plains extend from Kansas City, Missouri, to Denver, Colorado. At first the land was just a place to cross on your way to California or the Oregon Territory. Many died in the crossing. The mortality rate for children five and under was a staggering 25 percent. Besides wagon trains leaving Independence, Missouri, there was the Pony Express. It crossed the prairie from its starting point in St. Joseph, Missouri. Over the years though, a number of people stopped short of the coast, settled the prairie, and turned it into the world's breadbasket.

In this book there are five sites in the area that I visited and investigated. Two are in the Kansas City metro area and one each in Oklahoma, eastern Nebraska, and eastern South Dakota.

Argo Hotel

This quaint and remote little two-story red brick hotel is a surprisingly busy place. Crofton, Nebraska, is almost a ghost town. The railroad is just a memory here now and the highway is something that bypassed them, still the Argo Hotel is a beehive of happy activity.

Some of this activity comes in the form of the paranormal type. It is thought this activity emanates from the days this building had another use, that of a cancer sanatorium.

There are supposed to be at least three ghosts at the Argo. They probably are all from its hospital days. One is the spirit of a woman who was named Alice. She died in childbirth during the 1940s. Her spirit has been seen, felt, and heard. People claim to have seen her in the basement. People also feel a tap on the shoulder but when they turn to see who wants their attention, there's no one there. What Alice is most known for is calling out for her dead child.

Another ghost is only heard and has never been seen. It is the spirit of a baby heard crying at night. An historical note that enters here is during the building's last major rehab in 1994, a burlap sack was found sealed up in one of the walls. In the sack was found the bones of a baby. Are the baby's bones, the crying spirit, and the ghost of Alice all connected?

Another ghost was probably a doctor or staff member of the hospital. The owner and a co-worker saw him once. The apparition

Argo Hotel.

looked human, not smoky, was about 6 feet tall, and wore a white hospital gown. He was seen walking in a hall. He stopped, turned, and entered another room. As he did, his head made an extra turn and made eye contact with the witnesses, then turned away and closed the door behind him. The owner immediately went down the hall and opened the door. There was no one there.

The spirits seemed to have literally come out of the woodwork when the structure was rebuilt in 1994. Besides the baby skeleton found within the walls, there are a number of stories of workers quitting during the time the building was being gutted. The best story is about a telephone company employee who had been sent to set-up the hotel telephone system. He had no previous knowledge of the building's alleged spirits but he had plenty of information by the time he left. He was working alone in the basement but couldn't shake the feeling he was being watched. Next the lights started flickering off and on, and then he felt something go by him. When he turned, he came face to face with an apparition. He immediately ran out of the basement and refused to go back alone. He wasn't able to give a good description of the ghost; he hadn't hung around long enough to get a good look.

Phenomena reported by guests and staff include cold spots, flickering lights, glasses that shatter, and doors slamming without cause. The most active areas are said to be the basement and Room 11. Photographs of orbs are commonly reported here. While I was there, several people touring and using digital cameras picked up a number of various sized orbs.

During my stay, all I experienced was a good time.

The Argo opened for business in 1912. At that time Crofton was a booming railroad town. The hotel was a two-story brick structure with modern amenities. During its early years business was good at the Argo. In 1923, the hotel was sold and its name changed to the New Meridian Hotel. During prohibition it became a speak-easy with prostitution occupying part of the second floor.

43

They enjoy their ghosts here.

One claim to fame is Hollywood actress Leslie Brooks lived here during 1932 and 1933. At the time she was a teenager named Lorraine Geltman. She was a granddaughter of the owners and attended the Crofton School. Later she became a model and by 1941, she was in Hollywood acting in movies. Today the hotel has named a suite in her honor and memorabilia of her is spread through the hotel.

In 1935 the hotel was sold and converted into a health sanatorium. This phase of the building's history is very controversial. Many negative things have been written about the clinic. The current owner said many of the claims were outright lies. Past owners and employees of the building's clinics or hotel's family descendents still live in Crofton. The community is defensive and tight-lipped about the clinic. They say it helped a good number of people and are proud of it. They say it had modern equipment for its day and point out it had one of the first X-ray machines in the country.

What is known is the hotel was purchased by Joseph and Maria Wiefelhaus. Joseph was trained in massage and physical therapy. They came from Germany only a few years earlier. They remodeled the structure and expanded its half basement into a full length one, to provide space for various hot tubs used in therapy treatments.

The new business was named the New Meridian Sanatorium. Room and board were offered as part of the package. They treated people with chronic or terminal diseases such as arthritis, cancer, and emphysema. Patients came from miles around for treatment. The clinic prospered and at its peak had forty-two employees. But only one, the person who signed the death certificates, was ever an MD. I've been told since they didn't claim it to be a hospital but instead a sanatorium, this was legal and accepted at the time.

Some of the treatments such as massage, steam, and hot mud baths would have and did help relieve some people who came with arthritis. Others, such as those who came for colon cancer treatments were probably beyond anybody's help in those days of medicine. Much has been made about the number of dead coming out the back of the building at night, but even in these days of modern medicine, many people die in hospitals. Of course the bodies go out the back door. This is common procedure at hospitals and for obvious reasons. It doesn't imply anything sinister. With so many of the clinic's patient cancer cases, the mortality rate here would have been high, no matter what or how hard the staff tried. Many did die here, that I confirmed.

The sanatorium closed sometime in the 1950s for unconfirmed reasons. The building was vacant for a number of years until Dr. Charles Swift bought it. He converted it into his residence and doctor's office. He practiced there until his retirement in 1987. He was a very popular man in the community. The building lay vacant again for a few years. Then in 1994, it was purchased by its current owners. They gutted the interior and thoroughly rebuilt it. They brought back its original name, the Argo Hotel and had their grand opening on December 31, 1994.

The hotel has a great restaurant. Don't bother to drive back to the town on the highway; the food at the Argo is fantastic. On weekends there is live entertainment. There are two bars, one on the first floor with the restaurant and a second in the haunted basement. The hotel owner is a fun and entertaining character of a lady with a pet bird that did enough tricks for a floorshow.

Investigative note: A majority of the field interviews for this site were conducted in the first floor and basement bar areas. I can say with some authority they make a good drink here.

Contact Information
211 Kansas Street
Crofton, NE 68730
402-388-2400 • 800-607-2746
argo@gpcom.net
www.theargohotel.com

The Elms Resort and Spa

This is a resort with an interesting history, a bright future, and enough alleged spirits to keep a good number of ghost hunters happy.

The Elms Hotel.

The most interesting spirit here is a shadowy apparition. It has been seen in the ballroom, the lobby, downstairs poolroom, and on the grand staircase. It has even been photographed. What's so interesting is people claim that it's about 10 feet tall! After that, the next four ghosts are almost mundane.

Well maybe mundane isn't the right word. Another spirit appears as a body of a man floating lifelessly in the basement lap pool. During prohibition, gangsters used that part of the hotel for all-night drinking and gambling parties. The spirit is said to be that of a man killed at one of these illegal parties. It was thought to have been a mob killing or gambling dispute or both.

There are supposed to be a pair of spirits on the third floor. One is a maid in a 1920s style hotel uniform. Both guests and staff have seen her. It is claimed that besides the occasional prank on one of the cleaning crew this spirit mostly just watches the staff. It is thought she is just trying to make sure they are doing their jobs correctly. The other phantom of the third floor is disembodied footsteps of a small child running down the halls.

The last ghost I found stories of is said to be of a woman in great distress. She is supposed to be looking for her lost child. I suggest she try the third floor. She has even been accused of pulling people's hair and of throwing things across a room on occasion.

Most of the staff I interviewed had at least one story of unexplained sounds, showers turning themselves on, and even two who had seen "the shadow." The basement poolroom is said to be the most haunted part of the hotel. Staff have two ghost photos behind the lobby counter. The resort ghosts have been the subject of a number of newspaper articles, a mention in a book about Missouri ghosts, and the subject of an ongoing investigation by a paranormal studies group (www.ospri.net).

What originally attracted people here were the Excelsior Springs and their alleged health benefits. The first Elms Hotel opened for business in 1888. By all accounts it was a beautiful hotel. A fire destroyed this attractive structure on May 8, 1898. While no one was injured, the building was a complete loss. It was immediately decided to build a new hotel on the same spot but construction did not actually begin until 1908. The new Elms had a second grand opening in July of 1909.

The hotel caught fire again less than two years later, on October 29, 1910. The fire was so intense that it ignited an explosion in the basement boiler. The hotel was a total loss and again it is said that no one was hurt. A check of the guest list confirms half of this. There is one story that a maintenance man was killed in the basement during the boiler explosion. Some say it is his spirit that casts the giant specter seen around the building. The story of the maintenance man casualty has yet to be confirmed.

The hotel was completely rebuilt from scratch, yet again. This time fireproof Missouri limestone was used as the principle building material. This is the Elms you see today. Its third grand re-opening was on September 7, 1912.

During the 1920s the hotel was allegedly used by a number of gangsters, including the infamous Al Capone. It is even claimed he had a small number of "business meetings" in the boardroom. The basement was used as a makeshift speakeasy for all night drinking and gambling parties.

The next economic downturn for the hotel came during and due to the Great Depression. The hotel was even temporarily closed for a period of time. However, the

The structure has a unique architectural style.

with Truman election and presidential memorabilia.

In 1966 the hotel took another financial hit when the U.S. government ruled that mineral water treatments would no longer be covered by insurance. The hotel structure was allowed to decline to save maintenance expenses. The hotel closed in 1970 and remained as such for the next eight years. For the next two decades the hotel went through various owners, business models, refurbishings, and Chapter 11. Then after one more set of owners and a top to bottom interior rebuild, the Elms had yet another grand re-opening in July 1998. My tour of the hotel found that this rebuild was thorough and well done. The rooms here are quite attractive, along with the lobby, ballroom, lap pool, and restaurant.

Elms is where Harry S. Truman spent the 1948 general election night. He went to bed thinking he had lost the election. His aides woke him in the wee hours to inform him of his upset victory. Today the room is a suite named in his honor. This suite is nice, well laid out, includes a hot tub, and is decorated

The lobby has a lovely tile floor and an eye-catching 1931 Model A for a conversation piece. I had lunch at the restaurant and enjoyed my meal very much. Management was both friendly and helpful. I was given an extensive personal tour then allowed to roam, photograph, and interview at will. Just imagine how nice they must be to paying customers!

The Elms Hotel is the major landmark in the town of Excelsior Springs and is also listed on the National Register of Historic Places.

The resort has 152 rooms and suites. Facilities include two restaurants – one currently being remodeled, two lounges, a ballroom, gift shop, a fitness room, an indoor European style lap pool, an outdoor pool, a challenge course, a walking trail, and a volleyball court.

The Elms is located thirty-two miles northeast of the Kansas City Sports Complex. So if you're visiting the Kansas City area you may want to consider the Elms for lodging. The town of Excelsior Springs is a living relic of the Victorian Age and worth a visit. Both the city of Excelsior Springs and the management of the Elms are planning to once again market their spring water. The town has over twenty mineral springs. One major problem is that conventional water filtration plants remove many of these desired minerals. New ultraviolet water

cleaning technology is being planned that would leave them in. Put this together with America's interest in bottled water and health awareness and you have a potential boom. They could sell it bottled and use it as a draw for the whole town.

Over the years, the Elms has had its share of famous guests including President Harry Truman, gangster Al Capone, oil baron Harry Sinclair, and American artist Thomas Hart Benton.

Contact Information
401 Regent Street
Excelsior Springs, MO 64024
816-630-5500
800-THE-ELMS (843-3567)
www.elmsresort.com

Hotel Savoy

Built in 1888, Kansas City's Hotel Savoy is the oldest continuously operating hotel west of the Mississippi River. It is a place rich in history, a history that includes at least two ghosts. One of these ghosts that supposedly haunt the Savoy is that of Betsy Ward. She was an elderly woman who lived in Apartment 505 when the building was a residential hotel. She died of a heart attack while taking a bath.

The Hotel Savoy. Credit: Hotel Savoy.

She seems to have formed an attachment to the apartment and especially the bathtub ever since. Residents of that apartment have reported that the shower curtain pulls itself closed and then the faucets turn by themselves spraying water into an empty shower.

In September of 1990, one resident of the apartment, Larry Freeman, had this happen four times in one day. After the fourth time he went down to plead with the manager who was at a complete loss at what to do or say.

After that the manager noticed that the sounds of a radio turning itself on and doors opening themselves would come from Mr. Freeman's apartment even though he was gone at the time and had left the place locked.

Another ghost is said to be of Fred Lightner. He had owned an apartment at the Savoy with his wife Kathy.

In 1987, Kathy and her friend Reid Shaylor claimed to have seen his ghost. Mr. Shaylor, who was a writer and resident of the Savoy, crossed the hall to lend Kathy a cup of sugar. At that moment they both saw the gray transparent but still recognizable specter of Fred standing just outside his old apartment.

There may be other ghosts. Residents and past hotel staff have reported a lot of the usual phenomena of ghostly voices with no apparent source, strange footsteps in the hallway, doors opening on their own, and appliances going berserk. In recent years such activity has quieted down. In fact, the staff I interviewed had no personal experiences to report. They admitted knowing the stories associated with the Savoy but they had strong doubts that their hotel was still haunted.

The lobby is worth a visit. Its use of marble, stained glass windows, Corinthian columns, and old caged front desk are a trip in a time machine. The room that houses the Savoy Grill is even more stunning than the lobby. What really sets the room off are the famous Savoy murals. They were painted in 1907 by Edward Holslag and depict different pioneers leaving Westport, Missouri, and their trip west on the Santa Fe Trail. This room also has stained glass windows along with a beamed ceiling, luxurious booths, and beautiful ornate light fixtures. The restaurant's food enjoys a great reputation but is admittedly pricey, by my standards.

The building is on the National Register of Historic Places and has been used in film scenes for at least two movies, *Mr. and Mrs. Bridge* and *Cross of Fire*. A few of the famous people who were guests of the Savoy include Presidents Teddy Roosevelt and William Howard Taft, humorist Will Rogers, comedian W. C. Fields, and oil baron John D. Rockefeller.

Contact Information
219 West Ninth Street
Kansas City, MO 64105
816-842-3575 • 800-728-6922
info@savoyhotel.net
www.savoyhotel.net/

Stone Lion Inn

To obtain some of my information for this section I personally interviewed the owner, Becky Lucker, at length. Then I stayed the night at the inn, alone.

The Stone Lion Inn is an Oklahoma bed and breakfast that claims to offer its guests more than just a breakfast. Amongst the things this bed and breakfast offers is a weekend murder mystery theater with guest participation, a dining room that offers fine food for all three meals, a chance to spend the night in a former funeral home while you're still breathing, plus a few friendly spirits.

The Stone Lion Inn.

The inn was originally constructed as a residence for F. E. Houghton and his large family. He and his two wives had twelve children (his first wife died). To accommodate his large brood he ordered the most expensive house that Guthrie, Oklahoma, had seen up to then. It was an 8,000 square foot, four–level mansion and he could easily afford it. Mr. Houghton was the founder of the Cotton Oil Company and owner of the first car dealership in Oklahoma. These businesses would have made him a wealthy man in his day. Another benefit of the new house was that it was next door to their old house and thus it made for an easy move. Construction started in 1906 and was finished in 1907.

Still, by the 1920s the family had fallen on hard financial times. This was caused by a combination of boll weevil infestation and prolonged drought damaging the cotton crop. The house was leased to the Smith's Funeral Home and it was then used as a mortuary. As was common at the time, the Smiths lived upstairs above the business. What was the embalming room is now the inn's kitchen. The actual embalming table now serves as the inn's bar. The Houghtons moved back in the 1930s and Mr. Houghton died in the house late in the decade. The inn has been the subject of an investigation by

an Oklahoma paranormal group and the TV show *Ghost Hunters*. The building stayed in the hands of the Houghton family until 1986 when it was sold to Becky Lucker. She and her sons then converted this grand old mansion into a bed and breakfast. It was during this time that the building's ghosts were first publicly reported.

There are allegedly three ghosts here. Two are the spirits of people that are known to have died in the house. The first is the spirit of a little eight-year-old girl. She was one of the Houghton's daughters.

The Houghtons had just moved in when their daughter, Irene, came down with whooping cough. It is claimed that in caring for the little girl, a family maid overmedicated her with cough syrup. As was common in those days, the medication contained strong doses of codeine and opium, and this caused the little girl to die of an overdose. Guests have claimed that they suddenly notice a little girl in their room and she tries to tuck them in! Other reports are that she wakes guests by jumping on their beds between 2:00 and 2:30 a.m. One more

repeated claim is that she wakes guests in the morning by patting them on the cheek. In these last two examples, when the guest awakes, the child has disappeared. These occurrences have happened even when no children are checked into the inn. There are many other manifestations of Irene. These include numerous sounds, such as a girl giggling, footsteps of little feet running in the halls and up the back steps, and the racket of a wooden ball rolling on the hall floor. Previously it had been reported the little girl had been named Augusta. That was incorrect. New research revealed Augusta lived to the ripe old age of eighty-three. A search of census records showed an Irene Houghton in 1900 but none in 1910 at this residence.

When Becky Lucker first bought the building she didn't think ghosts, she thought intruders. While staying at the inn doing its renovations, the Luckers would hear the sound of doors opening and closing on the upper floors. Late at night there were also the sounds of footsteps running up and down the back stairs. More footsteps were heard walking the third-floor hallway. The

If these two lions don't scare you, maybe what's inside will.

The old embalming table is now used as a dry bar.

first couple of times Becky Lucker called the local police but no intruder was ever found. Eventually Becky stopped calling the police. One more phenomenon that let them know they weren't alone involved a closet full of toys on the third floor. One of Becky Lucker's sons used it to store his toys. Even though he dutifully put them away every night, morning would frequently find them scattered about the floor. It was only after a visit by some of the Houghton children did an explanation for the noises and the scattering toys come forward. The children lived on the third floor. The closet is where Irene and some of the others kept their toys. They had loved running on the steps, especially the ones in back and Irene used to roll her wooden ball down the third-story floor.

The third floor is now used for storage. When I went upstairs to investigate the haunted closet I found there were six closets to examine. Based only on my "feelings," I chose which closet I thought was "the" closet, then went downstairs and asked the owner. I had guessed correctly. One out of six; not bad guessing.

The best stories of the little girl, though, come from other children. The cook and head housekeeper, Michelle Smith, would bring her daughter Ebony to work. She would hear the girl playing and assumed her daughter's conversations were with an imaginary friend. When she asked her daughter who she was talking to, Ebony replied, "The little girl, mommy. You know it was just an accident what happened to her."

Becky had much the same experience once with her youngest son. She noticed him hanging around the kitchen and suggested he go up to his room and play. He responded he would when the little girl was gone.

Another ghost is the "Laughing Lady." She haunts the Bridal Suite. Her apparition in a white dress has been spotted there at least once. She has also been seen in the second-floor hall. Her most common manifestation is a boisterous laugh at around 4:00 p.m. Her origins are unknown.

The third non-paying resident is the spirit of Mr. Houghton himself. He died in one of the bedrooms during the 1930s. Today he lets his presence be known in a number of ways. One is the smell of cigar or pipe smoke where there is no one smoking. Mr. Houghton is seen although usually just out of the corner of the eye. Guests have identified him when shown his photo. When spotted, he frequently is in a suit and tall top hat. He roams the whole house but his favorite area appears to be the basement. In fact most of the help do not like the basement and refuse to work there.

Even though it wasn't public knowledge in the community, the mansion had a reputation in the neighborhood as being haunted even before it opened as a bed and breakfast.

The third floor of the house is said to be the most active area for the spirits. Paranormal groups claim to have photographed orbs, picked up EVP (Electronic Voice Phenomena) readings of a young girl and of an old man, and registered numerous cold spots with electronic thermometers during their investigations.

The inn does murder mystery dinner packages on the weekends and is open as a simple bed and breakfast by reservation during the week. A good breakfast is provided. I can attest to that; mine was excellent. I came on a Thursday and was allowed to spend the night alone. I slept on the first floor so I could hear the cook arrive and knock on the door at 7:30 a.m. It's a good thing I chose the first floor; doors kept slamming all night on the second floor. I attribute this to a combination of a drafty old house and a severe windstorm. My only other experience occurred on a walk through the house. I entered one first-floor bedroom and without touching a switch, the light came on. Then while I stood there pondering it, the light went off. I called the owners and asked if this had happened before and she said, "Yes." I next asked her if she knew how it happened. Again she said, "Yes," then added the words, "Motion detector."

The small municipality of Guthrie still has room for yet another haunting. This is the well-documented old Territorial Governor's Mansion. The ghost here seems to be quite friendly, it supposedly yells, "Hello." As long as you're in town you might as well check it out and get two hauntings for the price of one.

Contact Information
1016 West Warner Avenue
Guthrie, OK 73044
405-282-0012
StoneLionInn@aol.com
www.stonelioninn.com

The (Alonzo) Ward Plaza Hotel and Suites

The Ward reminds you of the opulent, big city, grand hotels of a bygone era, only done in miniature. The building is a solid six-story brick structure. Squat, tight, and cozy, it sits on a corner of the old downtown district. It was the pride and joy of businessman Alonzo L. Ward. The Ward opened on May 15, 1928, but alas, poor Alonzo was not to enjoy his beloved hotel for long, as he died in January 1929. Today he and a few guests don't seem to want to leave.

The Ward Hotel.

Alonzo had owned another hotel on the same site. He opened the first hotel in 1897. It was a three-story one-hundred-room place called the Ward Hotel. It was destroyed by a fire on Thanksgiving Day 1926. Alonzo quickly replaced it with another. The new hotel was bigger, more opulent, and supposedly fireproof. I use the word "supposedly" because the term "fireproof building" always reminds me of the story of the unsinkable ship. This time the place was named the Alonzo Ward Hotel. From then until 1964, the Ward family owned the hotel. Since then, ownership has changed hands several times.

During my investigation of the hotel I examined the basement. Previously it had been an apartment and at an even earlier time, a meat locker. Now it is used for storage but is being remodeled into a recording studio.

Entering the basement I was greeted with the smell of fresh paint and plaster and the sight of scattered tools and building material. There was even the sound of someone going through a box of tools. My lucky day, people rehabbing haunted buildings frequently have interesting stories. So I called out and walked towards the sound. Then the thought came to me; just who might be working on a Friday night?

The basement is a small collection of rooms

and halls; still finding the source of the noise was difficult and the workman didn't seem to hear my calls. I thought the workman was moving in front of me because the sound of the jingle of tools always seemed to be just around the next corner. Finally I came upon where I started. I had made a complete circuit of the basement and could not find anybody or any explanation for the noise. After giving out one more call and still receiving no response, I began to wonder if this just might be one of the hotel ghosts. As it turned out The Ward has spirits to spare.

There are reports of five different ghosts here.

The day desk clerk was said to have many interesting stories, so, I made arrangements to come back the next day to interview her. Next, I checked out the establishment's restaurant, then proceeded to leave till morning. On the way out I decided to look over the art gallery attached to the lobby. As it turned out it was a fortuitous stop. The art gallery owner turned out to be a nice, informed, and conversant gentleman. He had more tales than I have room for in

this section. He owned a condo and lived in the building. He claimed most tenants had their stories but usually kept them amongst themselves. They don't like the kind of attention one gets living in a haunted building. Still this gentleman was willing to share and I was the richer for it. One story involved hearing voices outside his kitchen window on numerous occasions. That doesn't seem like much until you realize he lives on the sixth floor! His doorbell rings and when he answers no one is there. A check of the security cameras catches no pranksters either. Alarm clocks reset themselves to different times. There are cold spots, items that appeared to have been moved, TV channels change on their own, and lights suddenly dim. Some of these things can be passed off as electrical problems of an old building but not all; besides most of the wiring was redone in the building's major rehab of 2004.

The main and most active spirit is said to be that of Alonzo Ward, still making sure that all is just right in his hotel. Another ghost is that of a man who committed suicide. During the 1930s a man described as "depressed"

Even though the building has been thoroughly reconstructed, it still maintains much of its old charm.

checked into a room on the fifth floor, opened the window, and took a nose dive onto Main Street. It is his spirit that is supposed to cause most of the events on the upper floors. Even more tragic is the couple that haunts the ballroom. They were a newlywed couple and had their reception in the ballroom. They died later that night in an auto accident. Today people claim to still spot them waltzing together on the dance floor. A common story about the room, and one that also happened to the art gallery owner, is that the piano will play on its own.

During one wedding reception in the ballroom the men's room door became stuck. Eventually a locksmith had to be called in. When he opened the door no one was in the room. All windows were closed and latched down from the inside. The bathroom door had been stuck because it had been locked with a deadbolt lock from inside the bathroom. Was this the ballroom couple pulling a prank? I went up to check out the ballroom and it is a great room for a party or reception just as long as the piano doesn't play on its own, or the men's bathroom door doesn't decide to lock itself. I didn't experience anything in the ballroom but did get something like the scent of perfume on the second floor. At first the smell threw me then I noticed a vase of flowers just down the hall and went to give them a sniff. They were plastic. There was no scent in this part of the hall either. I walked back to where I had smelled the perfume and the scent was still there. I found the scent existed at just one spot in the hall, in front of Room 230, and had no apparent source. With nothing left for me to do, I went to dinner. I would finish the investigation the next day with an interview with the day desk clerk.

The interview turned out to be worth the day's wait. Like the rest of the staff I met she was very friendly and professional in behavior. Also, like many of the staff, she had more than a couple of stories to tell about the ghosts. Phenomenon she reported included door knobs turning in people's hands, chains from ceiling light fixtures twirling on their own, lights turning off and on by themselves, and elevators moving to different floors on their own. Scariest of all, being touched on the shoulder and when you turn to see who wants you, no one is there. She also told me of a lady ghost that had been seen. They think she had been a guest. She haunts the second floor where she has been seen in the hall and also Room 230—the same place I had smelled the perfume the night before.

The hotel has been remodeled but still contains much of its original charm and décor. A few items, such as the 1920s switchboard and a booth to send telegrams in the lobby, really take you back in time. This is still an operational hotel, although the upper floors have been converted into condominiums. In deference to the condo owner, the staff will no longer say which room was used for the suicide on the fifth floor. It had been considered the most haunted room of the hotel.

The hotel has a ballroom, bar, and restaurant, which are closed on Sundays, and a high-end art gallery. The restaurant offers fine dining and just might be the best in town. The building is on the National Register of Historic Places.

Amongst the more famous guests of The Ward were President William Howard Taft, Senator John F. Kennedy, and comedian Jack Benny.

Contact Information
104 South Main
Aberdeen, SD 57401
605-725-5550
www.alonzowardhotel.com

Mississippi Valley

The Mississippi River Valley is both a geographical and historical boundary. It divides the country both physically and in time.

It has been both an obstacle and a highway. The traffic first consisted of canoes, then flat boats, next the steamship era, followed today by barges. It is a land of towering river bluffs, soaring eagles, and lush green farms. It is also has humidity, mosquitoes, and floods.

The spring of 1804 and St. Louis, Missouri, are the beginnings of American western history. This is when and where Lewis and Clark would launch their voyage of discovery of the newly acquired Louisiana Purchase. The expedition wintered on the east side of the Fathers of Waters. Their expedition would open the vast west to American settlement.

St. Louis claims the title, Gateway to the West, and the Gateway Arch National Monument is dedicated to the westward expansion.

In this section, just like the rest of the book, I only deal with locations on the west side of the Mississippi. There are two locations that are old mansions converted into grand bed and breakfasts and each is in walking distance of the Mississippi River. One is in Hannibal, Missouri, and the other in St. Louis, Missouri. Both cities were busy river ports during the steamboat era and St. Louis is a center for Mississippi River barge traffic today.

Lemp Mansion

Ranked as one of the top ten haunted houses in America and easily the most haunted place in my hometown of St. Louis, is the notoriously famous and ornately beautiful Lemp Mansion. It is the frequent subject of local TV and radio programs. Both national TV programs and paranormal groups have investigated the site. But the Lemp Mansion revels in its haunted history.

Doing research for this book I found volumes had been written about the multimillion dollar Lemp business, the cursed family, and majestic mansion. It covered a fair number of good writers with decades of research and still there are unsolved mysteries and a great deal of contradictions. This section is just a cross sample of the reams of information that's out there in public domain about anything named Lemp.

The first publicized ghost story about the mansion was reported soon after Charles Lemp's suicide in 1949. The house was sitting vacant and a few neighborhood teenaged girls snuck in for a look at the famous place. They got more than they bargained for. They decided to go upstairs and started up the main staircase only to be met by a Lemp coming down. They said the apparition was an older bearded man and described it as a human shaped puff of smoke. They never made it to the second floor, instead they ran out screaming.

The Lemp Family Mansion.

Sometime later the mansion was sold and converted into a boarding house. During this period some tenants complained of strange noises, disembodied footsteps, unexplained shadows, and doors slamming. Such rumors made it harder for the boarding house to attract tenants.

In 1975 the Pointer family bought the mansion and started to convert it into a restaurant and dinner theater. The structure was in a state of severe decay and needed major restoration in addition to the business conversion work. During this reconstruction period, workers claimed a good number of strange and unexplained experiences. These included tools that had been moved or vanished, slamming doors, strange noises, and the feeling of being watched.

One famous story that has been retold a number of times involves the restoration of a ceiling painting. The room had been a living room and was being converted into one of the front dining rooms. When old wallpaper was removed from the ceiling it revealed the surface beneath it had originally been an unfinished painting. It was decided to preserve the painting and an artist was brought in to restore it. One day while the artist lay on his back atop some scaffolding, he sensed somebody walk by beneath him. He felt that it was unhappy and didn't want him around. That was good enough for him. He left in such a hurry that he left his brushes behind. It was discovered later from a past Lemp family employee that William Lemp hated the painting. That's why it hadn't been finished and why it had been wallpapered over.

One spirit is the "Lavender Lady." She had been called that while alive and the nickname has stuck in death. She was William Lemp Jr.'s trophy wife. Her nickname was derived from her favorite color. It was virtually the only color she ever wore. Even her horse carriage and their rig were decked out in lavender. She became a sad figure in life and it has carried

An old hitching post in front of the mansion.

63

Will you find more than just a good dinner behind these doors?

over in death. Her sadness was caused by William Jr. openly cheating on her and their marriage. When her ghost is spotted it is claimed she appears sad and is wearing a lavender dress and broad-rimmed hat of the same color.

Another ghost is the Lavender Lady's ex-husband William Lemp Jr. and he hasn't lost his philandering ways. He had built a free-standing shower in one of the bedrooms in the mansion. Today it is part of one of the guest bathrooms used by the bed and breakfast customers. A few women have claimed and complained that they caught a man peeping at them over the top of the shower stall. It always turns out that no one was nearby to steal a peek and when shown photos or portraits they pick the likeness of William Jr. as the culprit.

Another Lemp that has refused to leave is Charles. Ghost hunters and clairvoyants have claimed to sense him and other times to have communicated with him. The apparition of a bearded man, in both human and spectral form, is said to be of William Sr.

The last ghost is the most famous and most controversial of the alleged spirits at the Lemp. He is called the Monkey Faced Boy. Spirit haunters say he doesn't like his nickname. He was supposed to have been the illegitimate child of William Lemp Jr. and one of the household staff. His nickname is due to his appearance and his appearance due to his affliction, Down syndrome. It is claimed that he spent most of his life in the attic, an area he haunts the most in his afterlife. He is supposed to have died in the mansion and was buried in the Lemp family burial plot. A lot has been written about the person and the ghost. The most controversial is that the child never existed. This is a major debate amongst a number of historians, ghost hunters, and writers.

The mansion was built in 1868 by Jacob Heickert. The location, while next to a brewery, was still on an exclusive block known as Mansion Road. Its official city name was 13th Street. In 1876 Heickert's son-in-law, William Lemp, purchased the house and so began the mansion's storied history. William Lemp was the owner of the Lemp Brewery Company. Mr. Lemp used the mansion as both a family residence and the brewery headquarters.

William Lemp inherited the business and a fortune from its founder and his father, Johann Lemp. Lemp helped introduce German light golden lager beer to America. It changed American beer drinking tastes and made Lemp a millionaire. He quickly replaced the first brewery with a much larger one to keep up with demand. This brewery was built atop Cherokee Cave. The cave helped chill the beer during the lagering process. This and other caves made St. Louis

a major beer-producing center before the days of refrigeration.

Johann Lemp died on August 25, 1862, and William took over the company. He immediately began a major expansion of the brewery, and he bought the mansion. It was a thirty-three-room Victorian manor. William immediately began to renovate and expand the place. This included building a tunnel from the basement of the mansion

The old brewery still looms over the neighborhood.

to the brewery cave. Parts of the cave were enlarged and converted to non-beer uses. There was an auditorium, a bowling alley, a concrete lined pool with hot water piped in from the brewery, and a theater with a spiral staircase leading to Cherokee Street.

I've actually been there and seen the old pool. The place is barely recognizable. The pool is now filled in with mud. For me, the place's history only added to the dark, ghostly atmosphere. The trip was decades ago and an example of urban spelunking. The area is now closed. Entry is by special permit only.

With the turn of the century, the family turned even richer. Still the new century quickly turned tragic for the Lemps. During 1901 Frederick Lemp, William Sr.'s favorite son and heir, apparently died mysteriously of sudden heart failure at the young age of twenty-eight. William Sr. was never the same. Depression finally overtook him and he committed suicide on February 13, 1904, by shooting himself in the head with a .38 caliber revolver. No suicide note was ever found.

William Jr. took over the company and the mansion. He was not the same man as his father. He spent a great deal on the mansion but ran both the company and his marriage into the ground. He had numerous affairs, including with the staff. He had prostitutes over and would have nude drunken swim parties at the mansion's cave pool. Beer was brought over from the brewery via the connecting tunnel.

Lillian continued on playing her role dutifully as mother and trophy wife. To help keep her busy and out of the house, William Jr. allotted her $1,000 a day for shopping. Just one catch, if she didn't spend it all, William would cut her off and she wouldn't get anymore. In 1909 the couple went through a scandalous divorce. Edwin, one of William Jr.'s sons, moved away and estranged himself from the Lemp family at an early age. Later, he inherited the family art collection, documents, and corporation records.

In 1919 Prohibition finished the brewery company. During March of 1920 William's sister, Elsa Lemp Wright, committed suicide in her home at #13 Hortense Place. She shot herself but left no note. At the time she was the wealthiest heiress in St. Louis. In 1922 the brewery company's land was sold at public auction.

Next was William Jr.'s turn. He committed suicide with a single gunshot at the mansion on December 29, 1922. Again no note was left. His son, William Lemp III, also failed to see old age. He died of a heart attack in 1943 at the not so old age of forty-two.

Charles Lemp, Will's brother, moved back into the mansion during 1929 and made it his private residence. In May of 1949 he went into the basement with his dog. He shot the dog and then himself. A servant heard the gunfire, ran to see what had happened, and made the grim discovery. One thing different, this Lemp left a note. It said, in part, "In case I am found dead, blame it on no one but me."

In these last three suicides there are conflicting accounts as to whether these people shot themselves in their heads or their hearts. Also it is claimed by some that there was a fourth suicide in the mansion—one of the housemaids was pregnant by William Jr. and in her distress hung herself.

It was soon after the 1949 suicide that the ghost stories started and the building's life as a house ended and its life as a business started.

Today it is a restaurant and inn.

A great–uncle of mine used to be an engineer on a "switcher" locomotive for the Lemp Brewery. Credit: Raisch Family Photo, circa 1900.

A third mystery is why did Edwin Lemp have all the family records and more puzzling, artwork, burned upon his death? Much of the artwork had spent decades locked up in the Lemp mansion vaults. Could some of the art have been stolen? The rich buying stolen art and stashing it in safe areas is nothing new in history.

William Lemp Jr. seemed to have few scruples and Lillian was spending a $1,000 a day on whatever! It's just a guess but if correct, then Edwin's actions make sense—he burned the art to hide one more family scandal.

There are a good number of mysteries that reach out from the Lemp's past. One is of buried treasure in the mansion, cave, or brewery. I don't believe it for a second. It's just legend. Most of the fortune was simply squandered.

A second mystery is why so many suicides in the same family? Especially in a family that seems to have had it all. For that mystery, I wouldn't even try to guess.

This is a very interesting place to visit. Orbs frequently appear on pictures of the site. The mansion has a ghost tour that occasionally is interrupted by shadows, strange noises, doors opening or closing on their own, and even the occasional visit by Mr. Lemp Sr. or Jr. Every Halloween there is a costume party at the Lemp. A research group named Supernatural Investigations also gives tours, lectures, and even provides video cameras to those wishing to capture the experience. One tour even includes drinks

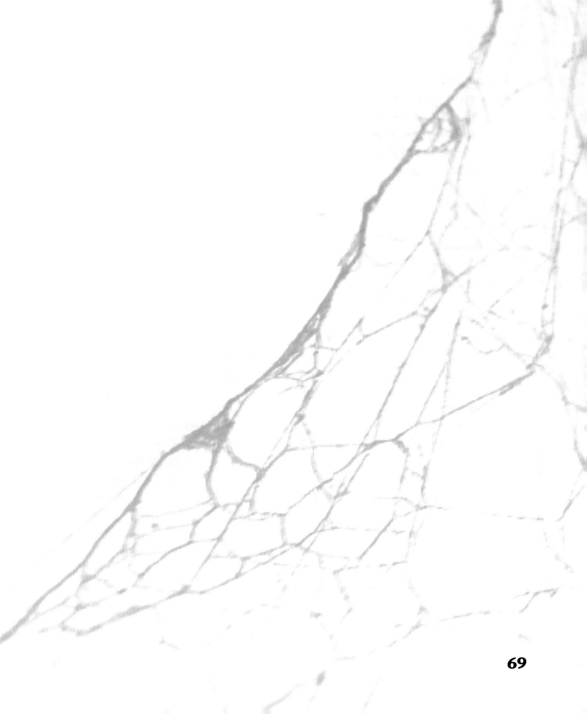

and appetizers. It is called the Lemp Mansion Experience. When I was there doing research one of the owners gave me his business card and it boldly states, "Famous from Ghost to Ghost." Their Sunday brunch is great and truly all you can eat.

Just two quick exits up the highway are downtown St. Louis, Busch Stadium, and the Gateway Arch. There is a very good history museum beneath the Arch and a train ride takes you to a viewing platform in the top. The Jefferson National Expansion Memorial was established in 1935 and is operated by the National Park Service. Its most well known attraction may be the Gateway Arch, but St. Louis's nationally historic Old Courthouse and the Museum of Western Expansion are also located on the site.

Contact Information
3322 DeMenil Place
St. Louis, MO 63118
314-664-8024
www.lempmansion.com

Rockcliffe Mansion

From its perch, high atop a rocky knoll, the Rockcliffe Mansion looms over Hannibal, Missouri. The center of Hannibal society in the early 1900s, today the Rockcliffe is a bed and breakfast with much to offer, such as a

The Rockcliffe Mansion.

spectacular view, special services, restored turn of the century luxury bedrooms, being on the National Registry of Landmarks, and a pair of ghosts. It seems the original owners loved the place so much they decided not to leave.

Over the decades numerous claims that the house is haunted have been made by live-in caretakers, housekeepers, guests, and owners. The 5 foot 4 inch frame outline of the first owner, Mr. Cruikshank, frequently appears in his old bed, always forcing the housecleaning crew to remake the bed yet again. Ghostly footsteps are heard to enter his bedroom. Both Mr. and Mrs. Cruikshank have been spotted in the dining room and the second-floor hallway. Mrs. Cruikshank is frequently seen in a black dress and still rings a bell for the servant. Guests claimed to have seen her floating in her old music room. Staff I interviewed claimed that photos have frequently shown orbs, wisps of glowing forms, and a number of Mrs. Cruikshank herself, including one of her sitting at the dining room table.

Nowadays, if you take the tour, leave your camera behind. The current owners do not allow indoor photography of their property. This 13,500 sq. ft. Colonial style mansion was constructed between 1898 and 1900. Its original owner was the lumber baron, Mr. John J. Cruikshank Jr. He moved into his dream home with his wife and four daughters. He died in his bed there in 1924. After his death, the family quickly vacated the house leaving 80 percent of the contents behind. It was boarded up and left vacant for the next forty-three years. During this period, caretakers reported unexplainable footsteps, noises, and the smell of cigarette smoke where there was no smoking going on.

In 1967, two weeks before it was to be demolished, the historic building was saved by three local families. They must have felt like archeologists opening a tomb when they first entered the mansion. Most of the original contents still lay where they were left forty-three years before, the only addition being decades of dust and cobwebs. For three floors and thirty rooms they stalked about as if on a treasure hunt. There were paintings, tapestries, antique furniture, clothing, personal artifacts, and much more. Most of these items are still there today, cleaned up and restored for you to enjoy. Restoration of this grand manor has been underway ever since that day. The site was acquired in 2005 by only its third owner. The new owners have continued with the building's historic preservation and renovation. The site has appeared in numerous books and has been investigated by paranormal groups. It is the centerpiece of the annual "Haunted Hannibal Tour." If

you are not able to stay but would like to see the mansion, they have paid tours.

Nearby is Mark Twain's boyhood home, the Mississippi River, and downtown Hannibal. Excursion boat rides are available on the mighty Mississippi and downtown Main Street is full of interesting shops and restaurants.

Contact Information
1000 Bird Street
Hannibal, MO 63401
573-221-4140
www.rockcliffemansion.com

Northern Rockies

The Rocky Mountains stretch from Mexico, across the western United States, and on into northern Canada. They get their name because they are literally quite rocky mountains. They are strewn with boulders, fractured rock, numerous talus slopes, and prone to landslides.

The abundant beauty of our Rocky Mountains lures sightseers from all around the world. They come in winter for skiing, snowmobiling, and other cold weather sports and they come in the summer for a whole different host of other outdoor activities. Laced through these rugged mountains are numerous inns.

Most of these inns rest in a beautiful setting and offer tremendous views and a few have that little something extra, like a ghost.

While in the area take advantage of the many unique and wonderful things to see and do. There are a good number of stunning national parks and monuments to visit. The mountain views and steam train excursion rides here are some of the best in the world. Be cautious of the high altitude, the tight winding roads, and the crazy mountain weather, which can include snow in August.

This section deals only with the northern half of the Rockies within the lower forty-eight states, minus the Yellowstone area, which is dealt within its own section in this book. I've chosen seven widely separated hotels for this section. Get used to it. Places in the American West are usually widely separated.

Ben Lomond Suite Hotel

Ogden, Utah's oldest, largest, grandest, and most haunted hotel is easily the Ben Lomond. Reports of ghostly experiences at this hotel go back to the 1930s. Six or more spirits are said to roam the whole hotel but the eleventh floor is by far the most active. Stories have come from guests, staff, cleaning crews, and construction workers during building rehabs. The construction workers seemed to have the most experiences in the shortest amount of time. The building underwent a major rehab in the 1980s during which some workers were reported to have left due to their unexplainable experiences.

On my visit there in 2008 it was undergoing another major reconstruction and once again the workers had their stories. The main ghost for them, and in all the source material I read, is that of Mrs. Eccles. Her phantom has been seen roaming the halls and in the third-floor fitness room. She has been seen by guests, construction workers, and security guards. I was given a two-hour tour by a construction site supervisor, Richard Hauley. He was a nice young gentleman who shocked me by knowing who I was. Turned out, he read my first book and was a fan.

I found out that Mrs. Eccles had been giving him and his crew a difficult time. One story involves a radio or jambox. The crew likes to play music while they work. Maybe Mrs. Eccles didn't like the music, whatever, an unseen force picked up the radio and threw

The Ben Lomond Hotel.

it, smashing it in the process. They also commonly smelled the scent of her lilac perfume. In fact during the tour when we got off the elevator at the third floor there was the scent. It lasted only a few seconds as if someone wearing it had walked by. The supervisor said this was common on the third floor and that's why he brought me there.

The eleventh floor has a whole treasure chest of hauntings. Topping the list is Room 1102. The ghost of a bride still occupies the place. She drowned in the bathtub on her honeymoon night. Reports of the room from guests and staff talk of cold spots, being shoved by an unseen force, the bathtub mysteriously filling with water on its own even when the room is empty, and the phone ringing late at night with nobody on the other end of the line. Even more odd is the adjoining room, Room 1101, is alleged to be haunted by the woman's son! When he heard of his mother's death, he checked into the hotel and committed suicide by jumping out the window of Room 1101. People claim to have seen the outline of someone lying in the beds of both Rooms 1101 and 1102. Mr. Eccles's brother is also said to have jumped to his death from the eleventh floor, sometime during the 1930s.

Room 1106 is yet one more allegedly haunted spot on the floor. The legend here is a woman was awaiting the return of her son from U.S. military service during WWII. She moved to the Ben Lomond and was living in Room 1106 at that time. After hearing of her son's death she passed away. From there the story diverges in three different directions. In two of the stories she dies in the room. One death is due to a broken heart and the other story is she starved herself. The third story is she died elsewhere but came back to haunt the room.

During my tour I became instantly ill upon entering the eleventh floor. I was dizzy and nauseated. I recovered just as quickly when I left the eleventh floor and this was before I knew most of the floor's history.

Other reported ghosts include the apparition of a man in Room 1010; a shoving spirit in Room 1212; in the tunnel, a ghost of a vagrant who died there; and the spirit of a

The structure towers over the city of Ogden.

night manager that was murdered in the lobby. Research confirmed that in 1976 a manager had been stabbed forty-four times by a fifteen-year-old assailant late one night. The manager died in the lobby and all for only $370.

One last story involves the elevators. Guests and staff report that elevators take off on their own, stop at the fifth floor, and then the elevator is filled with the scent of lilacs. Other manifestations include orbs, slamming doors, cold spots, and hearing people moving and talking in vacant rooms.

The hotel used to have haunted tours but these were suspended when the building was partially converted into condos.

The hotel started as the Reed Hotel. It was built by E. A. Reed during 1890 and opened in 1891. It was of brick construction and four or five stories high. In 1927 it was bought by a banker named A. P. Bigelow. Most of the original structure was raised and a high-rise tower was constructed on top of it. The new building reopened as the Bigelow Hotel. Mr. Bigelow went bust in the Big Crash of 1929

and in 1933 sold the hotel to the Eccles family. Once again, the hotel underwent a major renovation. This included building a penthouse on the twelfth and yes, thirteenth floors for the new owners, Mr. and Mrs. Eccles. At the same time the name of the hotel was changed once again. The new name was the Ben Lomond Hotel. The name was taken from a mountain in the Scottish Highlands that Mr. Eccles liked.

After the Eccles family sold the hotel it went through a series of owners and almost as many name changes. This included another major rehab in 1984. Eventually the building was bought by the RSH Corporation, and the name was changed back to the Ben Lomond. The hotel was closed in late 2001 and after more renovations reopened on New Year's Eve 2003. Part of the building is now condos and most of the hotel rooms are suites. As of 2008 the renovation was ongoing. The building is listed on the National Register of Historic Places.

An interesting point in the hotel's history is that in its early days it was a mob hangout. In fact Al Capone used it on his western "business" trips. There was a speakeasy in the hotel's basement. Besides the illegal drinking there was prostitution here. It is alleged that two of the workingwomen were even murdered. A tunnel ran from the railroad station under the street in front of the hotel to its basement. The tunnel was used during prohibition to run liquor into the speakeasy and to offer an escape route for mobsters in case the authorities showed up. Many cities had such tunnels during prohibition. Later the tunnels started to attract vagrants. Today the entrance to the tunnel in the hotel basement is sealed off.

The rooms at the hotel are very nice. Most are suites. A breakfast buffet comes with the room. There is an exercise room on the third floor; the one Mrs. Eccles likes to visit. The first floor has the lobby, a gift shop, a restaurant, and a bar.

The hotel is in downtown Ogden and as such is well located for those on a business trip. Also, Salt Lake City is just a short hop away on the interstate.

Contact Information
2510 Washington Boulevard
Ogden, UT 84401
801-627-1900 • 877-627-1900
www.benlomondsuites.com

Brown Palace Hotel and Spa

The Brown Palace Hotel and Spa has a great deal of glamour and history, it also has a small cast of characters for ghosts. The most prominent and active of these alleged spirits is the one of Denver socialite, Mrs. Louise Crawford Hill. From 1940 to 1955 she lived in Room 904 of the hotel.

During a major renovation, a hotel historian conducted a series of tours of the top two floors of the building. This was the area where permanent residents like Mrs. Hill lived. During the tour he told a number of stories including ones about Mrs. Hill's life and the extreme heartbreak she suffered because of a lost love. At the same time these tours began, the hotel switchboard started receiving calls from Room 904. When staff answered the switchboard they would only hear static from the other end of the line. What makes this more astonishing was Room 904 was empty at the time for the renovation (or was it?). The room had no occupant and had been emptied of its furnishings, including its phone. When the tour guide dropped the stories about Mrs. Hill, the phone calls from Room 904 stopped.

Most other spirits reported here seem to have been past staff. One is an apparition of a uniformed waiter who is seen in the service elevator. Another is of a train conductor. He was seen in the part of the hotel where the railroad ticket office had been located.

The Brown Palace Hotel is surrounded by a forest of steel and glass.

My favorite story is of a formally dressed string quartet playing music in the main dining room after hours. An employee went to investigate the unexpected music and found the well-dressed group. When he informed them they weren't supposed to be in there, they casually replied, "That's ok, we live here." With that, the employee left confounded. The room where this sighting is claimed to be used to be a music room known as the San Marco Room. It was where bands and other entertainment played for the hotel's guests. This included a group named the San Marco Strings.

Other non-staff spirits some have claimed include the disembodied sound of children playing in the hallways and a baby's cry deep in the hotel's boiler room.

The hotel's excellent downtown location makes it well situated to serve the business traveler. The building is designed to fill the street it rests on and it does a good job of it. Still, the hotel looks out of place as it is surrounded and dwarfed by looming modern steel and glass skyscrapers. Once inside the Brown you forget where you are and immediately become lost in the lobby's great beauty. It is six tiers high with surrounding balconies and capped by a stained glass skylight. Out of all forty places in this book, the Brown easily had the grandest and most attractive lobby.

The staff didn't treat me like a poorly dressed, bearded man asking a bunch of silly questions at a high-end hotel. They treated me like a preferred guest. Any staff I met were either in uniform or a suit. Whichever, the last thing they had put on in the morning was a smile. They also all came equipped with firm and friendly handshakes.

Contact Information
321 17th Street
Denver, CO 80202
303-297-3111
800-321-2599
www.brownpalace.com

Elk Mountain Hotel

Sitting on the banks of the Medicine Bow River at the foot of Elk Mountain is the small, elegant, and historic Elk Mountain Hotel. The compact establishment is overwhelmed by the beauty of its setting.

When I entered the hotel a feeling of precognition overwhelmed me. After introducing myself to the manager I felt compelled to ask, "Pardon me, but is your hotel haunted?" The manager was stunned and taken back for a moment, but then stuttered out weakly, "Yes." I replied, "Tell me about her." Again, the manager was stunned. This is how the rest of the morning went. The ghost, that is the first one we talked about, was a woman named Mary Evans. She was the wife of the first owner of the hotel, John Evans.

Numerous guests, staff, and most of the building's owners claimed to have seen Mary. When the current owners rebuilt the place they noticed that pictures would be moved but only ones of Mary. The old black and white photographs decorated many rooms but somehow or another would end up back in Mary's old room in a dresser drawer with a Bible on top of them. They tried many spots for the pictures and when they weren't moved from a spot, they figured that's where Mary wanted the picture.

Going with my gut feelings, so to speak, I said to the slightly nervous manager, "Mary's

The Elk Mountain Hotel.

room is on the second floor. Please show it to me." I was right again. Her favorite room is on the second floor, Room 10. The manager kindly took me to the room. Upon entering I noticed a rocking chair next to a window. I pointed at it and said to the manager, "This was her favorite chair and she used to look out the window from it." The manager informed me my guess was again correct and proceeded to tell me more "Mary" stories. Sometimes she is seen in the rocker and other times the chair rocks on its own even though no one visible is sitting in it. Mary seems to think she still runs the place and she runs a tight ship. She turns off lights left on and closes doors left open. Maybe that's why the owners don't feel the need to spend the night there. When you check in they give you a phone number to call during the night in case of an emergency or some such thing that would need their attention.

According to the manager a couple checked in one day, were given the phone number, and informed they would be alone in the hotel. Later that evening while in their room they heard noises coming from down the hall. The couple got up, went to their room door, opened it, and looked down the hall towards the direction of the noise. At that moment they saw a woman in old-time dress come out of Room 8, stroll to Room 10, and start to walk in. Then she stopped, turned her head towards them, and gave a cold disapproving stare. With a bit of a huff she then turned, went into Room 10, and closed the door behind her. The man, shocked and curious, went

This is a place with as much charm as it has history.

down the hall and knocked on her door. After receiving no answer he opened the door and found the room deserted. At this point the couple used the phone number. They explained they were not alone. When the owners convinced them that no other

John and Mary Evans. Notice, Mary won't even smile for her picture.

people were in the hotel, the couple checked out.

At the end of the tour I noticed a wall at one end of the lobby, it must have contained at least fifty photos. One picture contained a woman in Victorian period dress. Her smile-less face contained a pair of black eyes that looked right through you and followed you wherever you moved. I turned to the now quite nervous manager, pointed to the photo, and said, "This is Mary." She nearly fainted. Then I gently said, "Now tell me about the little girl." Her jaw dropped in amazement. There is a second ghost and it is a little girl. They don't know who she is, or was, but she is heard calling out on occasion. When you come to the voice that called out, you find yourself confronted with an empty room or staircase. Other times she is seen but not heard. She is seen out of the corner of the eye or just turning into a doorway. The cook saw her once in the lobby staring out the window. At the end I asked, "Can you tell me about the basement?" The manager grasped her chest in horror and pleaded, "What's wrong with the basement?" I just shrugged and mumbled, "Oh, nothing." I didn't have the heart to tell her.

There used to be a dance hall adjacent to the hotel. The dance hall was built in 1880 and it was expanded in 1920. It was purchased in January 1947 by Mark Johnson. After a remodeling, he opened it for business in the spring of 1948 under the name, Garden Spot Pavilion. He used the dance hall to bring in groups from the Big Band Era. The bands arrived by train, stopping here from Denver on their way to Salt Lake City, and stayed at the hotel. The Garden Spot lured some prominent entertainers such as Louis Armstrong, Les Brown, Tommy Dorsey, Harry James, Gene Krupa, Lawrence Welk, Tex Williams, and many more. The first-floor reading room at the hotel has autographed photos and other memorabilia from those days.

The first businesses here were a stagecoach station, the Overland Stage Station, and tavern named, The Crossing. The Elk Mountain Hotel was built in 1905 by John S. Evans. When first built, it had sixteen guest rooms on the second floor, and a tavern and restaurant on the first floor. The hotel was closed in 2000 and went through a complete rehab. It reopened in May 2002. There are now twelve rooms, all with a private bath. There is no longer a lounge but the restaurant serves alcohol, including fine wines and imported champagne. I had brunch and the food is quite good. The grounds have been landscaped and the old interior has been entirely refurbished. The original ornate embossed tin ceilings have been restored and give the place an old charm. The interior is a cross of country and Victorian. The building is listed on the National Register of Historic Places. One last brag for the hotel is that it rests on the banks of an award-winning trout stream, the Medicine Bow River. The hotel and the tiny hamlet of Elk Mountain are tucked away together in southeast Wyoming, 3.1 miles south of I-80 at exit 255.

I recommend you go for the fine food, good service, and beautiful setting. I just can't promise Mary will let you have a good night's sleep.

Contact Information
P.O. Box 54
102 East Main Street
Elk Mountain, WY 82324
307-348-7774
www.elkmountainhotel.com

Part of the hotel's beautiful setting.

83

Jameson Inn

Situated in the center of a picturesque mountain town is the small yet elegant tourist hotel, the Jameson Inn. When the hotel first opened, it catered to a different clientele, that of rough and tough working men such as miners and lumberjacks. The business had billiards, drinks, and prostitutes. In fact, prostitution was a major business in Wallace, Idaho, until the 1980s. A large number of working girls would have passed through the doors of this hotel and one even came back to stay. She worked in a harsh business; still it did not keep this woman from falling in love.

Her heart was lost to a man, and her true love's name is lost in time. Now it's her soul that's lost and roams the floors of the Jameson awaiting the love of one who promised to return. She called herself Maggie. Many of her clients were miners. She fell in love with one of them and when he struck it rich he said he wanted to marry her. First he would go back east, buy a house, get established, and then send for Maggie. She waited longingly for years but no note ever came from him. Finally she took matters into her own hands and boarded a train east to find her man. She never made it. She died on the train. Where she was buried, no one knows but they say her spirit came back to the Jameson and has been there ever since. Often guests claim to see a young woman in Victorian clothing sitting, brushing her hair in Room 3 or leisurely walking down the stairs. Sometimes her figure is seen strolling the third-floor hall in a long flowing dress. Her spirit always gets the blame for things that go whacky, such as when people are sometimes locked in their rooms or bathrooms on the third floor. Maggie has even been accused of tripping the electrical breakers when she's unhappy.

The Jameson Inn.

Some employees have even refused to go up to the third floor unaccompanied.

Maggie isn't alone here though. Workers and guests have both claimed to have heard loud, boisterous parties going on in the saloon during the late night hours. When somebody goes to investigate all they find is an empty room but the noise continues as if piped in by a sound system. This combination of all sound and no sight so unnerved one worker that he immediately fled the spot in a sprint and never returned.

The Jameson Inn is an attractive three-story brick structure. The first floor contains the business office, the kitchen, a restaurant, and a stylish saloon. The saloon has ornate ceiling fans, polished brass, and a long mirrored back bar. The second floor has banquet and private meeting rooms. The third floor has six bed and breakfast rooms. The management of the hotel is proud of their "Maggie" and have included her in their promotional brochure.

A couple of doors from the Jameson is the Oasis Bordello Museum. It is a fun and interesting museum dedicated to one of the major businesses in this town's history, prostitution. Some of the rooms on the second floor have been left as they were on the brothel's last day of business. There was a raid by federal agents and many people departed abruptly; some naked. In their haste, they left numerous items behind such as clothing, food, and personal knickknacks. Many of these things are still there today just where they were left. One more note, the museum is also alleged to be haunted.

Part of the building's elegant interior.

Another nearby haunted attraction is the Sixth Street Melodrama. Built in 1841, it is an eighty-six-seat theater that shows vaudeville melodramas. It too was a brothel at one time and it too is alleged to

The old railroad depot, part of picturesque downtown Wallace, Idaho.

Dante's Peak. The town looks like something from a Norman Rockwell painting. With its wide sidewalks, numerous museums, shops, and restaurants it's an interesting place to walk around. When in the area, I made a habit of stopping here and have always enjoyed myself. If you stop in Wallace, check out their claim to be the center of the universe. There is a lot more to see and do in town and the adjacent area. The surrounding mountains are stunning and loom so close they almost swallow the community. These mountains offer some of the best bike trails in the country. Nearby are the mining ghost towns of Burke, Gem, Mace, and Delta.

be haunted. Ghosts here do not confine themselves to buildings though. Stories abound of haunted mines occupied by spirits of those who died on the job and of lights bobbing at night on the mountainsides. These lights are supposed to be lanterns held by lost miners roaming the mountains looking for their final resting spot somewhere in a lost mine tunnel.

Wallace is a quaint and friendly town from another era. It is easy to see why Hollywood used the place as a film set for the movie,

Contact Information
304 6th Street
Wallace, ID 83873
208-752-1100
rshaffer@cebridge.net

Occidental Hotel

This was another location I just stumbled on. I was in Buffalo, Wyoming, seeing a client. It was a beautiful day. I had just stepped out the door of the bookstore and was enjoying the warmth of the sun on my face when I noticed this old, yet still beautiful hotel down the street. Something just tugged at me, inside, compelling me to check the place out.

It was a two-story brick structure tucked neatly into a row of buildings on an old part of Main Street. A sign above the front door proclaimed this old but handsome structure as the Occidental Hotel. I strolled through the front door and was surprised by the large size of the lobby for a small hotel. The lobby is an elegant step back into the Old West. Hat in hand, I approached the front desk clerk, and said, "Pardon me, but I have to ask, is your hotel haunted?" The reply came back, "Why, yes."

The spirit this hotel is best known for is that of a lonely little girl. The owners think her name was Emily, but aren't sure. She was the daughter of a prostitute and lived at the hotel with her mother. It is thought the mother had been a little too busy with her own life to provide much attention to the child. Emily died around 1900 of cholera at the tender age of ten.

Nowadays Emily is still trying to get a little attention. People claim to hear the voice of a little girl say, "Please hold me." She also touches people gently on the back of the shoulder. The owner I interviewed notices

They do serve bison here.

customers shrugging their shoulders then turning around having a puzzled look on their faces. At that point she knows Emily has just tapped someone on the shoulder again. This little spirit also adjusts mirrors, moves items, rocks chairs, and gets into anything hooked up to electricity. It is said she caused the smoke detector to constantly go off. A psychic was brought in and she said Emily wanted an orange cat. The owners went out and bought a stuffed orange cat and set it out for Emily. The smoke detector stopped malfunctioning. Emily occupies the south wing of the hotel. In fact, she is sometimes heard skipping through it.

The north wing has its own spirits. It is thought there is the spirit of a man and at least one of the madams. The man is said to be a little bit of a poltergeist and the madam is mostly sensed as a heavy and negative feeling. The area she occupies is not normally used by guests. I stumbled into the area while investigating the building and had an extreme oppressive sensation. I did not know the building's history yet, so it couldn't have been the power of suggestion. I turned to leave the area and noticed scratches going up the back steps. The marks had been caused by cowboys' spurs during the hotel's "cat house" days. Many customers had used the back steps to come and go then. The most haunted spot in the hotel is this area, Room 23, and the laundry room.

The hotel is old. It first opened in 1880. For at least the first three decades it was prosperous and well visited. Then time, traffic, and maintenance passed the building by. In 1986 it closed. In 1997 John and Dawn Wexo saved this historic building. For the next ten years they restored the hotel to its present elegance.

Although small and little known, this is an award-winning hotel that truly looks like a museum setting. Suites have private baths, and some even have brass beds. These rooms are both attractive and comfortable. The lobby is true western décor and well preserved. There is a well-stocked saloon with an old billiard room and live music on Thursday nights. The restaurant has an interesting menu and offers both inside and outside dining. There is a small library for guests. The old barbershop has been converted into a nice bookstore and gift shop.

Old hotel registers are on display in the lobby and bear such famous signatures as Tom Horn, Ernest Hemingway, Herbert Hoover, T. R. Roosevelt, William (Buffalo Bill) Cody, and under different names, Calamity Jane, Butch Cassidy, and the Sundance Kid. It is claimed that Owen Wister stayed and wrote here for a time. This hotel is on the National Register of Historic Places.

For outdoor fun you don't have to go far. The town of Buffalo rests at the foot of the Big Horn Mountains and the Big Horn National Forest.

Contact Information
10 North Main Street
Buffalo, WY 82834
307-684-0451
www.occidentalwyoming.com

Stanley Hotel

The Stanley is renowned for its stunning setting, its grand elegance, and its rich history, but it just might be the most famous for its ghosts. It is said by some to be most haunted hotel in America.

This is a hotel that revels in its ghostly notoriety. The ghosts are the prime topic of the hotel tour. A list of ghosts is written into the hotel's brochure. Signs and posters telling of the spirits adorn the hotel's interior. The gift shop sells books, t-shirts, posters, videos, and other items dealing with ghosts, the movie *The Shining*, and the hotel's hauntings. I bought a coffee mug that has RedЯum written in blood red. The Stanley and its ghosts have been

The Stanley Hotel.

It's a great thing I love my work because the whole time during my research investigation at the Stanley the phrase "all work and no play makes Jack a dull boy" kept coming to mind.

featured on the History Channel, Discovery Channel, Travel Channel, and the SCI-FI Channel. There are so many ghosts and haunted rooms here you need a scorecard to keep track.

The main entrance to the inn.

Of all the ghosts, the most famous in life was the hotel's founder, F. O. Stanley. His spirit is most often seen in the lobby and in his favorite room when alive, the Billiard Room. It is claimed that he materialized in that room once during a visit by a tour group. He just suddenly appeared behind the last member of the tour group. He has been seen by both guests and staff. He is described as wearing a suit, derby, and a big smile. People have identified him as the ghost they've seen from photos taken of him during his life.

Not to be forgotten, Mrs. Stanley also still hangs around the hotel. She is credited with playing the piano in the ballroom and even more often in the music room that adjoins the billiard parlor. Guests or staff will hear piano music coming from one of the two rooms and with a bit of curiosity decide to see who's playing. When they check the place out many are greeted with the sight of a vacant room. Sometimes the piano keys are seen to move but when the investigating person approaches closer the keys stop playing. And a few other times the person is surprised by the apparitional figure of Flora Stanley playing the piano. At times the music has been loud enough for guests on the second floor to call the front desk and complain. During my investigation I was told by staff a photo had even been taken showing a glowing face of a woman at the piano in the music room. Flora has also been seen making a non-musical appearance. She has been observed walking down the grand staircase in a Victorian era dress.

In the inn's early days the fourth floor was where the hotel help used to live. In many cases they were families with children and the children played in the hall. Some say they still do today. Some of these "children stories" of the Stanley would end up in the book and movie, *The Shining*. It is claimed that Stephen King had a number of encounters with the children. One was the ghost of a little boy on the second floor calling out for his nanny. Another child ghost is that of Katie. She was a daughter of one of the hotel maids and supposedly died in the basement at the age of twelve. A TV series recorded a couple "hellos" and laughter I would call creepy, in the basement. The voice sounded like it was from a little girl. Children's stories from the Stanley that ended up in *The Shining* include the little twins that make such a terrifying appearance. In real life and in the book they were the son and daughter of a maid. They died of an illness while living in the Stanley. In the book they are murdered by their insane father. Some say Stephen King actually saw the ghostly pair during his stay. Others say he merely heard the story. Either way he found the two were perfect for the part. Another phenomenon used in the movie and attributed to the little ghosts is the red ball that comes rolling down the empty hall. For those who didn't see the movie, a little red ball comes rolling down the hall and when you look up, no one is there. Sometimes giggling is reported with the sighting. Steven King was said to have experienced this event.

During a winter while the inn was closed, a homeless woman broke into the unheated concert hall building and froze to death there. Since then her apparition has been spotted periodically, usually during the winter, in the building.

Another ghost is of maid Elizabeth Wilson. She helped make the Stanley famous. She occupies one of the most haunted rooms in the hotel, Room 217. She has been said to unpack people's luggage, hang up their clothes, and turn on the water in the room's bath. People say they leave the room for a short period and upon returning, their clothes have been unpacked and put away. Guests have left the room in a hurry in some occasions and other guests rent the room intentionally on an annual basis. The story around the hotel is Jim Carey stayed in the room for a total of a half hour before checking out without explanation. People would steal the number off the door of this room so often for a souvenir that the hotel now sells it in the gift shop.

Yet another ghost is that of Lord Dunraven. He haunts Room 407. It used to be his room and he thinks it still is. He owned the property the hotel stands on before it was

Is it a spirit orb or a photographic anomaly?

built. It is claimed that he stands in the corner of the room near its bathroom door and watches over whoever has checked in. The room's light switch is in that corner and Dunraven likes to play with it. In one case the room's occupants were bold enough to tell Dunraven to quit. It worked. He stopped flicking the lights off and on for the rest of the evening.

Another complaint coming from people, who have stayed in 407, is that they hear

the elevators late at night, and the noise was keeping them awake. The only thing was that the elevator was not in operation at the time. At other times a man has been spotted staring out the window of 407 and this when the room was supposed to be vacant.

Along with the fourth-floor hallway, the rooms that are reported to have the most activity are 217, 302, 401, 407, 412, and 418. Room 401 is the bridal suite and it is included in the hotel tour. While taking the tour and listening to the various ghost stories associated with the room I noticed the smell of gardenia. I asked the tour guide about the scent and she said the gardenia was the scent of a bride that had died in the room on her wedding night. The guide asked

if anybody else smelled the perfume and nobody did. To me the scent was strong and unmistakable. I had no prior knowledge of this ghost and her scent so it could not have been the power of suggestion. Additionally, I have bad sinuses and rarely detect odors.

Although some areas report more activity than others, phantom footsteps and ghostly apparitions have been reported throughout the hotel. One area of extreme activity is the attic. On a number of occasions guests staying on the fourth floor call the front desk and complain about the noise of people moving furniture on the floor above them. Staff is often at a loss trying to explain to the guests that they are staying on the top floor. All that is above the fourth floor is an empty, low ceiling attic. And the list goes on. In all, there are enough ghosts and ghost stories here to write a book about it.

The Stanley's founder and namesake was F. O. Stanley. He was the inventor of the Stanley Steamer automobile and it made him a fortune. There is a Stanley Steamer in the lobby of the hotel today. He came west due to his poor health on his doctor's recommendation. Stanley's journey took him to Estes Park, Colorado. He loved the area but found the town lacked amenities. Not doing anything halfway, F. O. Stanley built a grand hotel for himself, his family, and all his visiting friends. Construction started in 1907 and took two full years to complete. The hotel opened on the 4th of July in 1909. The doctor's advice seemed to have paid off. Mr. Stanley lived to the ripe old age of ninety-one.

Today the hotel is open year round. This was not the case until after the 1970s. Since then the whole complex has been rebuilt and restored to its original, yet improved, elegance. Today the complex is on the National Register of Historic Places. Presidents, Hollywood celebrities, and even the Emperor of Japan have stayed here.

Amenities include a well-stocked gift shop, guided tours, a restaurant and bar (the food is very good there), a snack bar in the basement of the hotel, a ballroom, and spa.

Spread out before you is the resort town of Estes Park and just a few miles away is Rocky Mountain National Park.

Contact Information
333 East Wonderview Avenue
Estes Park, CO 80517
970-577-4000 • 800-976-1377
www.stanleyhotel.com

This is the room where I smelled the perfume. Notice the wisp in the left of the photo.

The piano that Mrs. Stanley is said to play.

Virginian Hotel

Along a little used stretch of the old and historic Lincoln Highway is the even older and very historic hotel, the Virginian. It sits on Wyoming's high plain near the Medicine Bow Mountains. Another interesting thing about the hotel's location, it's in the ghost town of Medicine Bow. Both the town and the inn are a step back into a different time. The hotel is a National Historic Landmark.

It comes with a restaurant, a saloon, and "Ol' Hank." Previously I have reported the name of this ghost as Hal. I was incorrect. It was that I simply misunderstood.

The Virginian Hotel.

The Virginian Hotel and Hank were both something that I just stumbled upon while doing field research for a ghost town book. I was in Medicine Bow, Wyoming, and one of the few businesses still open was an old hotel; the Virginian. It was an impressive, stout, three-story, white stone structure. To my good fortune it had an air-conditioned restaurant on the first floor and was open for lunch. Great, a ghost town where you can get a cheeseburger!

While waiting for my lunch order, I decided to check out the hotel. Touring is encouraged by the establishment. When vacant, the doors to their beautiful rooms are left open for your viewing pleasure. It was like walking through a Wild West museum. I enjoyed myself thoroughly, while being quiet and respectful of the guests checked in behind the closed doors. Coming upon the third-floor landing I noticed the door immediately in front of me was closed but most others were open, so I chose to check them out. Beautiful traditional western style décor filled every room. I pivoted in the hall, walked back to the landing, and just as I was about to go back down the stairs, stopped in my tracks. The door that had been closed was now wide open. I thought it was strange that I hadn't heard a sound from anybody or the door either. I shrugged it off and looked the room over. Like the rest, it was beautiful but no evidence that anybody had just been in it. So I went back downstairs and had a good lunch; a cheeseburger and pie for desert. If a grizzly doesn't get me on one of my western adventures, my diet will. When the nice waitress gave me the check I took the opportunity to inquire about the area for my book. One question I asked, "Do you know of any other ghost towns in the area?" At first a puzzled look came over her face and then she popped, "Oh, you mean Hank?" Realizing her misunderstanding while at the same time being wildly curious, I replied, "No, but tell me."

This is the story she told me. Hank was a man who had checked into the hotel during its grand opening. He was at the hotel waiting for his ladylove who was supposed to be traveling there to be married to him. She jilted him and never showed up. She never even sent a note. He died in his room of a broken heart and his spirit still waits at the hotel for a love that will never come. Wow! Great story. Then I asked her what the ghost does at the hotel. She went on, "Sometimes you just get that feeling someone is there, watching you. That sometimes Hank moves things, turns light on

and off and, oh yeah, sometimes he opens or closes doors on you."

The place makes a great road stop. The cheeseburgers and the homemade pie at the restaurant made for a wonderful heart stopping lunch for me. The hotel also has a saloon. There is a western museum across the street from the Virginian. Nearby are five other ghost towns: Bosler, Coyote Springs, Rock Creek, Rock River, and Walcott. You can read more about these towns and Medicine Bow in my book, *Ghost Towns of Wyoming*. Also of interest in the area are the Como Bluff fossil beds.

Part of downtown Medicine Bow.

Contact Information
Highway 287, 404 Lincoln Highway
Medicine Bow, WY 82329
307-379-2377
virginianhotel@yahoo.com

The old Medicine Bow railroad depot is now a museum.

The Ozarks is a place where life intentionally moves at a slower and more relaxed pace. It is a land of old river levees, even older watermills, numerous tour caves, and giant springs. It is a large, weathered limestone plateau that is carpeted in forests of hardwoods, cut by clear running streams, and dotted with fish-filled lakes.

The area's name comes from the Ozark Mountains. It encompasses most of southern Missouri and northern Arkansas. The land is a paradise to the camper, fisherman, hiker, hunter, and spelunker. It also has the best canoeing in America. The Buffalo River in Arkansas and the upper Jack Fork River in Missouri are simply spectacular. One caution: the roads can have more twists than a plate of spaghetti. When driving in the Ozarks it will take longer than you think to get anywhere and you will be tired when you get there. Tip: take it slowly and plan a picnic stop along the way.

Arcadia Academy Bed and Breakfast

The Academy is a large complex of red brick buildings. It is of sturdy but obviously old construction all shaded under a grove of large hardwood trees. With its adjoining cemetery, it is a dark and foreboding place. The complex has been put to many uses over its 150 plus years. Today it is a small group of businesses. One of them is the Arcadia Academy Bed and Breakfast. The complex is full of history and something else—ghosts! There are so many alleged ghosts here its easy to lose count. They have been sensed, seen, felt, heard, and photographed.

The ghosts that are seen and heard the most, and even photographed, are the nuns. Many never left. They are still there today in the Academy's cemetery. If you visit the cemetery you will notice the nuns' graves are marked with three dates. The dates are when they were born, when they took their vows to be a nun, and when they died. The nuns have been heard singing in the auditorium or the chapel, when someone checks it out the room is empty. They have been spotted kneeling in the cemetery, praying in the chapel, and walking the grounds or hallways. It is said they even shush the guests that are loud.

The first time I was on the grounds of the Academy was during 2001. I had been canoeing and camping and was returning to St. Louis when I decided to stop for breakfast. I had heard good things about the bakery, one of the businesses here.

The magnificent chapel.

Being the curious type I gave the place a short tour after enjoying a great breakfast. The place sort of rambles on. There are numerous buildings with over two hundred rooms amongst them. I was on the third floor of the main school/dorm building when I found more than just a cold spot, it was a cold room. It might as well have been a meat locker. I asked the girl, "Excuse me ma'am, what did this room used to be?" She turned towards me and flatly replied, "The infirmary." I immediately stepped back out of the room.

The Academy's history starts in 1846 as a Methodist school named the Arcadia High School. The town of Arcadia was laid out three years later and named after the school. Later the school was upgraded to a college. During the Civil War, the Union used the complex as a hospital. This started mid-1861 and went on until the fall of 1863 when it reopened as the school.

In September of 1864, a Civil War battle passed through these grounds. Remains in the way of bayonets and bullets are still found in the soil there today. During the

The entrance to the old Ursuline Academy.

battle, the complex temporarily regained its status as a hospital. This is where the story of Civil War spirits at the complex originates.

In 1877 the Ursuline Sisters bought the property from the Methodist church. The campus slowly expanded over the next forty years. Then on February 9, 1917, most of the college burned to the ground in a devastating fire. The sisters simply rebuilt their campus, bigger and better than before. The school prospered for decades. Time and maintenance costs eventually caught up with the place. The last class graduated in May 1971. The nuns left in the 1980s—the Ursuline Sisters sold the property in 1992. The conversion to a retail establishment was then started.

The part of the complex with the Arcadia Bed and Breakfast.

On my last visit to the old Ursuline Academy, I found the Arcadia Academy Bed and Breakfast to have been closed. During an interview, the owner informed me that he hopes to reopen the business in the near future. Currently the complex is being listed for sale. In the meantime, there is a second bed and breakfast, Nostalgic Place, right next door. This second bed and breakfast is not haunted but staying there would let you view the exterior and walk the grounds, including the cemetery of the old Ursuline Academy. In fact the building the Nostalgic Place occupies was originally part of the Academy complex. Today this building and the lot it rests on is a separate business operation from the Arcadia Academy. The structure served as the Academy's laundry operation and is claimed by its owners to be the oldest surviving building of the complex. The owners have completely rebuilt the structure and turned it into an attractive and comfortable place to stay. Breakfast comes with the room. Their telephone number is 573-546-1201.

Until its recent closure, the Arcadia Academy had an antique store, a beauty shop, restaurant, the bed and breakfast, and a bakery. I can attest that the food at their bakery was wonderful.

Nearby are numerous Ozark streams, Missouri State Parks, and the Mark Twain National Forest. The combination provides numerous opportunities for a wide variety of outdoor activities. Also close at hand is the historic site of Fort Davidson. It's a Civil War fort and battlefield that is said to contain its own spirits. The place's history will surprise and even shock you. It is well worth a visit.

Contact Information

200 South College Street
Route 1, Box 4b
Arcadia, MO 63621
573-546-4249
www.arcadiaacademy.com

The chapel and attached Academy building.

Crescent Hotel and Spa

In it's one-hundred-plus year history, the Crescent Hotel has been known by several colorful nicknames such as the "Grand Old Lady of the Ozarks," the "Queen of the Ozarks," and my favorite the "Most Haunted Hotel in America." After seeing its long list of alleged ghosts you can understand the hotel's third nickname.

The Crescent Hotel.

It is said the hotel was already haunted the day it opened. A man who died during the hotel's construction didn't bother to wait for the grand opening to check in. He had already made Room 218 his home. Later, when the structure was converted into a hospital, many more spirits would make the building their permanent home.

My research found stories of eight different ghosts that supposedly haunt the grounds of this resort. The most infamous would be Michael. He was an Irish stonemason who plunged to his death from the roof during construction in 1884 or 1885. He fell where Room 218 was eventually constructed and has never left the place. It is now called the "ghost room," although at least four more rooms are claimed to contain spirits.

In Room 218, Michael is said to cause the TV to act strangely, pounds loudly from inside the walls, makes other strange noises, and turns the lights on and off. Some have heard his final falling cry. One story is his hand is seen coming out of the bathroom window. If that's not enough, sometimes the room's door will open and then slam shut locking in guests or cleaning personnel. Staff often blame Michael for unexplained happenings on the second floor. They even talk to him at these times. For example, a member of the staff that cleans on the second floor told me her vacuum cleaner would turn off. She thought maybe the plug had come out of the outlet but upon checking, found that the vacuum was still plugged in. When she turned to go back, the machine came back on by itself. After this happened several times, she called out, "Ok, Michael, that's enough," and the problem stopped.

Another spirit is said to be of a little girl. Her apparition appears late at night in one of the rooms. She doesn't do much; she just stands at the end of the bed and stares at you. I got this story from the ghost book the hotel keeps behind the lobby desk. The information was in a letter mailed to the hotel from one of its guests.

One more ghost is a former patient by the name of Theodora. She occupied Room 419 in life and has stayed on in death. Sometimes she is seen although most times just her voice is heard. Cleaning personnel, workmen, and guests have all experienced her. In fact, a few claim to have even conversed with her. She says she was a cancer patient in the hospital. What's more is that she knows she's dead. She died in the hospital but claims to love her room so much she stayed behind. She also claims to have many friends who were patients in Baker's hospital and they all enjoy being

together at the Crescent! It is claimed she has taken the clothes of guests and thrown them out in the hall when they have complained about her room. During my investigation of the hotel I tried to take a picture of the door to Room 419. No matter how many times I pushed the shutter button, my camera simply refused to work. Then while standing there, exasperated, the camera would simply go off on its own, even though I wasn't touching any of its buttons. This happened three times in a row. After that I said, "Please, come on, I just want to take a picture." I tried again and this time the camera worked!

Today's front entrance.

103

Yet another ghost is of a formally dressed gentleman who has been seen in the hotel even before "The Baker Days." He has a beard and mustache and wears Victorian era clothes. He is most often spotted in the lobby at the bottom of the staircase. It is thought it is the spirit of Dr. Ellis, the one time hotel physician.

Another ghost is of a young woman who either jumped or was pushed to her death from the rooftop balcony. A student did fall to her death there when the building was a girls' college in the early 1900s. Some said she had been depressed and committed suicide. Another story is she was pushed and the suicide was a cover story to protect the school. Her ghost has been seen roaming the garden, standing on the balcony she plunged from, and worse, actually seen re-enacting her death fall.

My favorite reported ghost is the nurse. Her appearance often is simply bone chilling. She is seen in her white nurse's uniform pushing a gurney. People report even hearing her footsteps and the wheels of the gurney squeak. As it moves down the hall the whole apparition simply fades away from sight. The event is supposed to occur after 11:30 p.m. when Dr. Baker had the dead bodies moved to the hospital's morgue.

Then of course there's Dr. Baker. His ghost is seen in the lobby wearing a purple shirt and white linen suit and in the old morgue wearing a white surgical gown. He is also seen in his old office in the fifth-floor penthouse.

One last ghost is known as the "Lady in White." She wears a white dress and is seen "floating" through the gardens or standing on one of the balconies. Maybe this "lady"

The attached white structure is the Conservatory Room.

is the same ghost attributed to the student who fell to her death.

Both the town and the hotel have a great deal of history. Eureka Springs was a booming resort town in the 1880s known for its healing mineral hot springs. The town still exhibits a great deal of physical charm from those days.

While the tourist boom was flourishing, the Crescent Hotel and Spa was built on the highest point of land in town. It was built with a foreboding look known as American Gothic. Construction started in 1884 and when it was finished in 1886, the Crescent was the grandest hotel in the Ozarks. It served as a playground and health resort for millionaires.

The hotel became famous and business flourished, but due to the building's high maintenance cost its profit margin was meager. The hotel was sold to the Frisco Railroad who used the building as a summer-only hostel from 1902 through 1907. The healthcare craze of bathing in spring water faded and American tourist habits changed; all of this doomed this high-end hotel.

In 1908 it became an exclusive all girls' boarding school while still operating as a hotel during the summer. Even with high tuitions, the building maintenance cost and a further decline in the summer tourist trade kept the operation from becoming profitable. The Crescent College and Conservatory for Young Women closed its doors in 1924. It reopened as a junior college during 1930–1934. Then the hotel was leased out over the summers on an individual basis until 1937.

During 1937, the building was leased by Norman Baker and converted in a cancer hospital. Mr. Baker went by the title of doctor, but he wasn't. What he was, was a charlatan. He had already been run out of Iowa and convicted in 1936 of practicing medicine without a license. He fled to Mexico where he ran a radio station and a cancer hospital. In 1937, when he acquired rights to the Crescent, he converted it into the Baker Hospital. He advertised that he could cure cancer without surgery, radiation,

The hallways looked like a Hollywood film set.

or X-rays. When he sent these advertisements out in the mail, authorities convicted him of mail fraud. The fake hospital was closed and Norman Baker was sentenced to four years in the Fort Leavenworth Federal Penitentiary.

Some sources claim that Mr. Baker used heinous means to cover up his fraud. This included shipping the terminally ill off to asylums for their last weeks of life, burying bodies in the walls of the basement, and running an incinerator at night to dispose of the numerous dead victims. Some stories even talked of bizarre experimental surgeries being conducted. Other sources claim these stories are only legend. Even if these last claims are only legend, Mr. Baker's crimes of taking advantage of the last hopes of the dying were horrific. If you look into these macabre claims, you will notice the same story lines appear in numerous horror movies. Question is who copied whom?

Because of the scandal and the approaching Second World War, the Crescent was boarded up and left to the ghosts. It stayed this way from 1940 to 1946. New owners then bought the establishment, restored it, and reopened it. In 1967 the hotel suffered a devastating fire. The fire destroyed the conservatory, the fifth floor, and most of the fourth floor. Smoke and water damage afflicted much of the rest of the building. In 1972 the hotel was sold again with the new owners doing another rebuild. The hotel reopened on May 1, 1973. Then in 1997 the Crescent was purchased by its current owners and they put the hotel through yet another restoration. This has been done in phases and is ongoing. The fourth floor was finished in 2000 and the conservatory in 2002.

The hotel has a number of services and special features, such as a spa. The hotel has a large dining room on the first floor along with a gift shop and an art gallery. The gallery has works from over eighty artists.

The Conservatory Room is located next to the gallery. The walls in the halls are covered with numerous framed newspaper articles about the hotel's history and ghosts. There is a combination lounge/restaurant, named the Baker Lounge, on the fourth floor. It is done in an art deco style, a style Dr. Baker liked. The lounge has a walkout-viewing balcony. Ghost tours of the hotel are conducted every evening for a fee.

The lobby has a fireplace and something unique for a high-end hotel, a cat. Frisco is a soft and friendly feline that is happy to share its house with you. Frisco just walked in the lobby one day and made itself at home. It isn't even the first one to do so. They had another cat named Morris who resided in the hotel lobby for twenty-one years and has even been put into the hotel brochures.

The hotel grounds and gardens are very well maintained and greatly add to the beauty of the exterior. Its location offers great vistas of the surrounding landscape. The various oaks and dogwood trees offer a rainbow of colors in both spring and fall.

Because of the numerous rebuilds, when you enter the hotel today, you are arriving at the back of the building. Take the time to see the front; it is a magnificent structure.

Below and all around the hotel is the resort town of Eureka Springs, Arkansas. The community has numerous restaurants, bars, gift shops, specialty stores, museums, and more. Many other places beside the Crescent are also said to be occupied by spirits. There are tours of both the town's historic and ghostly sites. When getting around town keep in mind the streets are narrow, winding, often crowded, and almost everything is either up or downhill. Also this is a resort town, it often has resort prices. Nearby are the Ozark National Forest, Beaver Lake, and the Buffalo River. This area provides some of the best canoeing, hiking, spelunking, and fishing in the country. It's also great for camping, outdoor photography, hunting, and many more outdoor activities.

Contact Information
75 Prospect Street
Eureka Springs, AR 72632
479-253-9766 • 877-342-9766
www.crescent-hotel.com

The hotel is surrounded by beautiful gardens.

The Parlor Bed and Breakfast

Another bed and breakfast located in the Arcadia Valley is the Parlor Bed and Breakfast. It is a magnificent house and in its lifetime has at least twice been an object of deep affection. The first time was when its first owner had it built for the love of his life. The second time was when its current owner bought the building, fell in love with it, and started rehabbing it to its original beauty. One more thing, for a short while it was also a funeral home.

The Parlor Bed and Breakfast.

REST INN PEACE
AT
THE PARLOR

EST. NOV. 11. 2000

They have an interesting way to market their business.

Today it is a friendly little inn with what the owner/manager refers to as "two friendly ghosts." In fact, Jeanne, the owner/manager, says the spirits leave her with a warm and wonderful feeling.

One is the spirit of a little boy and the other is of an old woman. The little boy is heard bouncing a small ball, but is not seen. His face has been seen looking in a second-floor window and once appeared playing at a customer's feet. The lady is more heard than seen. You may hear her dress swish as she walks past you. One guest whose alarm clock had not gone off, repeatedly heard a soft female voice gently repeat, "time to get up", until he sat up, then the voice simply stopped. A few guests claimed to have seen a woman out of the corner of their eye. Also unexplained disembodied shadows have been reported.

For years people claim to hear noises from unoccupied rooms. The first stories of ghosts in this house date back to the 1930s. The most haunted room is said to be the old master bedroom. Other alleged phenomenon are the doorbell ringing on its own, Christmas decorations turning themselves off, and clocks that won't keep time. More stories can be found in the guest remarks book at The Parlor.

The house was built by Charles Tual. He was an architect and wanted to build something special as a symbol of his love for his wife. He succeeded. The house has a two-story turret with the unique feature of curved glass windows. Construction started in 1901 and took to 1908 to finish. Amongst its old-time finishes were stained glass windows and

Tiffany lamps. During the early 1960s the house was used as a funeral home. Before being converted into a bed and breakfast, the house had set vacant for a few years. Today there are three rooms to rent and each is stuffed with beautiful antiques. Two rooms have Jacuzzis. A large hot breakfast is provided with any room.

For a while The Parlor was run as a murder mystery dinner theater and when it operated as such the owners kept a coffin in the front parlor. Although the coffin is no longer there the establishment's brochure headlines with the phrase, "Rest Inn Peace."

Nowadays, management has a different yet interesting way to attract attention. They offer two different and unique ways to tour historic Ironton and the Arcadia Valley. There is the horse and carriage method or, more inline with their name, you can tour in a 1974 Cadillac hearse. Even if you don't stay you can take one of the regular tours of the wonderful house.

While interviewing Jeanne, it became obvious that the restoration of this beautiful old building is a labor of love and it shows. The restoration work is meticulous and well done. This makes the second time the structure has been the object of deep and unabiding affection. While she is only one of the owners, she is the passion and driving force behind the business and the restoration of the fine house.

Nearby are the numerous activities and sites of the Arcadia Valley and the Mark Twain National Forest. These include hiking on the Ozark Trail, photography at Elephant Rock State Park and Royal Gorge Scenic Area, and historical recreations at Fort Davidson State Historic Site.

The Arcadia Valley is full of history.

Contact Information
203 South Knob Street
Ironton, MO 63650
866-550-6142
www.TheParlorBandB.com

The remains of Fort Davidson and site of a bloody Civil War battle.

Sage Brush Country

Sage Brush Country is what some call the broken land of southern Idaho. It is a place of prehistoric lava flows, disappearing rivers, and large desert springs. Even the area's parks, such as Craters of the Moon National Monument and Bruneau Sand Dunes State Park, are defined by the land. Scattered across this setting of pinion and rocks are desert mountains with thin forests of pines that reach up and beg the skies for rain. Here the sunlight reflecting off the sands not only bring heat but also a change in the color of the lands. Breathtaking vistas await the photographer and beg for a wide-angle lens.

When traveling the area off the interstate be aware it can be some miles between services. Take extra water and have a good map.

In this section I have three small, little known, yet still historic and interesting hotels.

Enders Hotel

Like all the other hotels in this book the Enders Hotel is old, historic, and haunted. What's unique about it is it contains a museum. A large one. Most of the second floor consists of the Soda Springs Idaho Historical Museum. The rest of the hotel might as well be a museum. Built in 1917, it has been restored to look today like it did back then.

The hauntings seem to have started or were at least first reported during the rehab of the building. Construction crews mentioned seeing shadowy specters or having the feeling of being watched, this was especially true in the basement. On at least one occasion a worker left the basement in fright, claiming to have seen a ghost, and refused to go back down alone. Had the construction disturbed the spirits?

The spirits seemed to have stuck around to bother the cleaning crew. When I interviewed them the majority reported the feeling of being watched, of doors opening and closing on their own, or their cleaning carts having been moved while no one else was on the same floor with them. They place the cart in front of the door of the room they are cleaning and start to tidy up the room. When they turn around, the cart is gone. They go to the door and see that the cart has been moved down the hall. One cleaning lady admitted, "This creeped me out."

The cleaning crew unanimously voted the basement the scariest part of the hotel. The manager showed me a picture taken in the basement during the building's rehab. Claiming it to be the hotel's ghost, it showed something of a shadowy figure. Then she shared an old newspaper article telling of a

The Enders Hotel.

killing in the hotel. On May 6, 1926, police shot and killed a guest of the hotel. (Some think the ghost is the man killed.) The man had gone insane and was running around acting demented and brandishing a razor. He had already cut himself and was ranting threats at any who neared him. When he lunged at the police they fired in self-defense and killed the tormented soul.

The hotel portion of the business closed operations during the 1970s. The café remained open on part of the first floor of the building. Ownership of the building changed hands and after a year of renovations the hotel reopened in July 2001. There are thirty bed and breakfast rooms to rent, complete with original antique hotel furniture. The hotel has a banquet ballroom, the Geyser View Restaurant, and a saloon.

Again the museum is worth a visit. Amongst its collections is a revolver that is claimed to have belonged to the Sundance Kid. The museum is on the second floor and occupies most of that level. There are also rooms to rent on the second floor and they have communal bathrooms. The rooms on the third floor have private baths.

The hotel gift store, which used to be a barbershop, has a more interesting inventory than the typical postcard and candy variety store of many other inns.

The surrounding countryside is a typical western setting of mountains and sage brush that blush when kissed by the setting sun. The town's main claim to fame is it has the world's largest captive geyser. Soda Springs is in southeast Idaho on Highway 30, between Pocatello and Bear Lake.

Contact Information
76 South Main Street
Soda Springs, ID 83273
208-547-4980
www.visitidaho.org

The hotel's restored lobby.

Idaho City Hotel

The Idaho City Hotel is historic, old, small and, oh yes, haunted. There are only two ghosts here but then again I did say it was a small hotel. The most important ghost is that of the business's first owner, Mary Smith. The owners have never seen her but guests and cleaning crew have. The way it usually happens is a guest comes to the front desk with a question or comment about "the old lady."

She is attired in period dress and said to be a little grumpy at times. One guest claimed to have talked with her and Mary said she was unhappy and in bad health. How much worse can your health get? You're dead! Another guest reported seeing her in a rocking chair on the front porch. Only trouble is nowadays there is no rocker on the front porch of the hotel.

One cleaning lady saw an older woman exit a room, cross the hall, and enter the room opposite it. When she went in that room to see who it was, the room was vacant. The ghost's favorite room is Room 1. She is seen entering it by people but when they open the door no one is there. The owners say they hear footsteps coming from the second floor above them, but try to convince themselves these are just old building noises.

The second ghost is that of a little six or seven-year-old girl. One worker had

The Idaho City Hotel.

several experiences with the little entity. For instance, one day the worker heard a sneeze and automatically replied, "Bless you" before remembering she was alone in the hotel at the time. Since then she has heard additional disembodied sneezes and giggles that she says sound like a little girl. Then one day while taking a nap in Room 1, yes it's the little girl's favorite room too, she felt somebody tickle her foot. When she looked up from her bed there was nobody there. Then, while fully awake, she felt somebody sit next to her on the bed. What she felt gave her the impression the entity she was experiencing was the size and weight of a small child. Who the little girl was is not known.

The site where the hotel stands today used to be the heart of Idaho City's Chinatown. The location had an opium den and a laundry. The log construction was rough at best and done in 1864 or 1865. The laundry stayed open until 1914. The building burned down sometime after that.

During the 1920s Mrs. Mary Smith bought the land and constructed a new hotel on the place. This is the Idaho City Hotel you see today. It is a two-story log and frame structure with a wrap-around balcony. It opened in 1929 and was how Mary supported herself and her daughter Nellie. At that time there was a dining room on the first floor. Mary lived in what is now Room 1. The rooms have private baths and are nicely adorned with antique furniture. The lobby is located on the west side of the first floor. It is small, obviously from another era, and frequently occupied by a dog that demands to be petted.

The town itself is a major tourist attraction. It started in the early 1860s as a gold mining boom town. At one time it was Idaho's largest city. When the boom went bust, the town almost faded away. During the 1960s it started to attract a good number of tourists looking for a bit of the Old West. There is a lot of history here with numerous historic buildings dating back to its pioneer days. There is an old pioneer cemetery on the edge of town and it is alleged to be haunted also. Some mining is still done in the area but logging, tourism, and outdoor

What's behind Door #1?

sportsmen are the major contributors to the local economy.

There is much to do in the area for the outdoor enthusiast. The place is surrounded by mountains, national forests, and almost a dozen mining ghost towns. The town has a visitor's center and a separate history museum that helps display and preserve the town's glory days. Both the hotel and the visitor's center have gift shops.

You can read more about Idaho City and its surrounding ghost towns in my book, *Ghost Towns of Idaho: The Search for El Dorado.*

Contact Information
P.O. Box 70
Idaho City, ID 83631
208-392-4290
www.idahocityhotel.com

Lava Hot Springs Inn

I was in Lava Hot Springs, Idaho, checking out the town's small history museum and while there asked a local business owner if he know of any allegedly haunted hotels in the county. His reply was a sharp, "Oh, you bet!" I asked where. Gesturing with his thumb he pointed over his shoulder and said, "The building behind me in the alley." So I decided to look it over. When I first saw the inn it was apparent that the building was built as a hospital, a TB sanitarium to be more specific. It was opened in 1925. Of course, there were a number of people that checked in the hospital but didn't check out. They died there and a few still linger around the place today.

One of these lingering spirits is Martha. She is usually spotted in Room 13, which is understandable; she died there. Many did. Room 13 used to be the surgery recovery room. Today it is one of the guest rooms and the old surgery is now the second-floor sitting room. Staff told me another room popular with the spirits is Room 10. An aerobics instructor was stuck in her bathroom because the sliding latch refused to budge no matter how hard she tried to move it. After awhile she finally gave up and the latch just slid open on its own. The door was finally open but the poor woman came unhinged. A massage therapist claims while setting up her table in the second-floor sitting room she felt something grab her leg. She turned and saw a disembodied hand had reached out from behind the curtains and had grabbed her leg. She ran from the building screaming.

The Lava Hot Springs Hotel.

One of a number of warm pools surrounding the hotel.

The town and the inn get their name from the nearby warm mineral springs. The hospital was constructed in 1925. The location was chosen because the area offers a combination of dry desert air and the warm mineral springs. The spring fed a warm mineral pool in the basement of the hospital. Today it is the breakfast room. The disease of tuberculosis, or TB, was little understood at the time and these treatments by themselves could not cure the illness. There was something of a quiet epidemic of TB during the 1920s and 1930s. The death rate at these hospitals would have been high. It was probably no different at Lava Hot Springs. The hospital morgue, and the side basement door where they took the bodies out, is just down the hall from where they now serve breakfast.

Starting in the 1950s the building was used as a rest home. After 1980 the rest home went out of business and the building remained vacant for the next seven years. New owners purchased the building in 1987. They converted it into the hotel and opened it for business in 1988.

A story the desk clerk related to me would make anyone scratch their head and question their senses. While at the front desk one afternoon he heard a car drive up and stop just outside his door. Then he heard the car doors open and a couple of voices engaged in conversation. Being a friendly host he walked outside to greet his new guests only to be met with an empty parking lot. I was also told that orbs have been photographed here, even in the dark.

The hotel is a three-story brick structure built to an art deco style. Most of the guest rooms are former patient rooms, of course. Warm mineral water feeds a collection of small pools that surround the hotel. These hot pools were added by the hotel owners during the early 1990s. The hotel has sixteen units to rent and breakfast comes with the room. The Jacuzzi suites were sweet. The town of Lava Hot Springs is located in the southern corner of the state of Idaho on Highway 30.

Contact Information
94 East Portneuf Avenue
Lava Hot Springs, ID 83246
208-776-5830 • 800-527-5830
www.lavahotspringsinn.com

Lucky #13?

Southwest

The American Southwest is much more than a land of sun and sand, cactus and coyote. It is also a land of rock canyons, snow-capped mountains, and pine forests. It is a place where both the temperature and food can both be hot. It is a place of booming cities surrounded by vast open areas. It is home to such wonders as the Grand Canyon and Meteor Crater National Landmark. Its name literally comes from its location in the southwest of the United States. For the purposes of the book it is used to designate the area in the states of Arizona and New Mexico. I have included three hotels from the first state and three hotels from the second state.

Copper Queen Hotel

This beautiful hotel is squeezed by desert mountains, narrow winding streets, and a dense pack of other buildings, all competing for your attention. Still, the Copper Queen finds a way to stand out. Located in the desert mountains of southeast Arizona

The Copper Queen Hotel.

is the old mining town of Bisbee. This community claims a good number of haunted structures including five inns. The most famous of these is the Copper Queen Hotel.

This hotel is credited with three spirits. The most famous and endearing of the trio is Julia Lowell. She was a prostitute that lived in Brewery Gulch during the early 1900s. Julia would entertain her guests at the Copper Queen. She had the misfortune of falling in love with one of her clients. This customer was a married man and when Julia told him of her love, he ended their business relationship.

Julia was so devastated that she committed suicide in one of the rooms she used at the Copper Queen. It is claimed that she still likes men. She is credited with whispering in men's ears, lifting blankets off sleeping men's feet and even tickling them. Some claimed to have seen her. She appears either as a puff of bright white smoke or other times as a very human, scantily dressed woman holding a bottle of liquor. Some men claim to have woken in the middle of the night and discover there is a half-dressed woman at the foot of their bed. She does a strip tease dance but when they reach out for her, she disappears. Maybe just a dream? She roams the whole building but her favorite area is the third floor. Today Suite 315 bears her name in honor of her spirit.

Another ghost is that of a little boy named Billy. At the age of eight or nine, he drowned in the San Pedro River. It is believed his mother or other relative was a housekeeper at the Copper Queen. It is thought he liked the hotel in life and came back in death to be both near a relative and in a place he felt comfortable. Today Billy likes moving or hiding small objects in some of the guests' rooms. Billy is supposed to predominately haunt the second and third floors. Most sources say he is never seen but his footsteps are heard running in the hall, accompanied by a child's giggle. Some claim they feel his presence or hear his crying, especially when they run the water in their bathtub.

The third spirit is that of an older gentleman. He is tall, bearded, and has long hair. He is dressed in a fine black suit, sometimes with a cap and top hat. Some claim to have smelled cigar smoke right before or after seeing him. Some say his name is Hal, but this isn't confirmed. He has been seen in the lobby, stairway, and third and fourth-floor hallways.

Other reported phenomena are orbs and slamming doors, particularly Rooms 212, 304, and 308. The Teddy Roosevelt and the Julia Lowell suites are said to be the most haunted. There are two journals with guest ghost entries at the front desk.

The Copper Queen Hotel is a gem and a great stay. I highly recommend their restaurant. The service and food were both excellent. The rooms are comfortable and surprisingly cool even when the air conditioning isn't on.

The hotel opened in 1902 after four years of construction. Building on steep, loose soil was difficult and the site had to be leveled first with dynamite. It was built for and by the Phelps Dodge Corporation. Since then it has been rebuilt and remodeled numerous times.

The building has beautiful light fixtures and a restored tin embossed ceiling in the lobby. The third and fourth-floor balconies are a great way to view the town. The hotel has an outdoor pool on the second floor. The restaurant has both indoor and outdoor dining. There is a saloon and it contains a one-hundred-plus-year-old portrait of Lily Langtry. If you want a haunted room call ahead and make reservations. While I stayed there, numerous calls came into the front desk requesting such rooms. The ghosts of this hotel have been the subject of a good number of newspaper articles, books, and least one TV program.

The streets of Bisbee are narrow.

Famous guests who have stayed here include the actor John Wayne and General "Black Jack" Pershing.

The town of Bisbee started as a copper mining camp in 1877 and boomed into a large community of well-built structures. Today some sources list it as a ghost town: it is not. It is well occupied by artists, business people, and tourists. It is an interesting, picturesque town with many numerous historical and architecturally interesting structures. Bisbee is worth a visit. Bring a camera and a broad–rimmed hat for the sun. The summers can be brutally hot, so most people visit during the winter or spring.

There is a tour of the town's haunted places given by a nice lady named Renee. Her business card proclaims her as "ambassador to the spirits." She was kind and patient enough to let me interview her twice. For more information, visit www. OldBisbeeGhostTour.com.

Contact Information
11 Howell Avenue
Bisbee, AZ 85603
520-432-2216
www.copperqueen.com

Gadsden Hotel

The Gadsden Hotel.

This is a rather large hotel for such a small and off the beaten track town. Still it has plenty to offer and attracts people from all around the country, many of them ghost hunters. It is claimed they have plenty to hunt at the Gadsden. Stories of the supernatural at this hotel go back for more than fifty years.

While doing research for this section it was difficult to keep track of all the alleged spirits. On the other hand it was easy to pick my favorite ghost story, that of the "Hanging Lady." She was engaged to be married, but her fiancé fell in love with another woman and ended the engagement. She didn't take the news well. She put on her dress and got on a public bus. She got off at the bus depot that used to occupy part of the first floor of the Gadsden Hotel. Then she went to the ladies room and hung herself. Occasionally her hanging body is still spotted dangling in the same restroom. This story was given to me by a desk clerk whose sister had gone to the restroom and seen the apparition. She left the room in a screaming flight. She later said what terrified her most was that the apparition didn't look like a ghost but looked human, "just like you and me."

That is the scariest claim about the ghosts of the Gadsden; they look like real people. Spirits here are often mistaken for customers or staff. This would make the hotel's most infamous ghost, "The Headless Man," a terrifying sight.

He has been seen in some of the hallways but has been mostly spotted in the basement. There are three different stories about this spirit. One story is he was a miner who hid a treasure in the basement and was murdered in the hotel. It is said he still wanders the basement either guarding or looking for the lost treasure. Another story is the apparition is seen in old khaki army clothing. The third spirit is rumored to be Pancho Villa looking for his lost skull. Not to be a party-pooper, but this is only a legend. Pancho Villa was assassinated in Mexico during 1923. The Gadsden burned down to the foundation in 1928 and was rebuilt and opened in 1929. Pancho Villa could never have been to the new hotel. Local legend says he was at the old Gadsden in 1927 and he rode his horse up the grand staircase. A chip in the marble staircase is said to have been caused by the hooves of his horse. Again, he was already dead. Research shows it is unlikely he was ever in Douglas, Arizona. The chip in the steps probably came from their fall into the basement during the 1928 fire. On my visit, staff said that the headless man hasn't been seen in a good number of years.

Another spirit that is supposed to have come over from the first hotel is the ghost of a ten-year-old Indian boy. It is claimed he came into the lobby around Christmas 1919, to see the hotel's large, decorated tree. When hotel personnel tried to remove him from the lobby, he ran from them. His flight took to the second-floor mezzanine where he fell over the rail to the lobby floor and to his death. His spirit is still seen occasionally running in the lobby or second-floor mezzanine. He is credited with flicking lights on and off and moving small items in guest rooms on this floor.

Other very real looking ghosts include Jonathan, a cowboy in the basement; a little girl who cries in a corner because she's lost; a cleaning lady who vanishes when she's talked to; and a tall middle-aged man who hangs around one of the laundry rooms. A security guard doing his late night rounds even had a gentleman pass through him when he tried to stop and question him.

There is one spirit that does make ghostly manifestations. It is a fluorescent apparition of an old, white-haired woman. A desk clerk I talked to saw her pass through a door while entering Room 104. This ghost has been reported everywhere from the basement to the top floor of the hotel. People have photographed this spirit and even claimed to have spoken to her. A photo of this Gadsden ghost even made an issue of *Arizona Highway* magazine.

There are more ghosts at the Gadsden than space allows me here. Other phenomenon at the Gadsden includes orbs in photos and video, the sound of disembodied footsteps running in the hall, and cold spots. The most haunted area seems to be the basement. The most active periods are claimed to be around Christmas and Lent.

I showed up on Easter Sunday. I made two tours of the building that day. The second took place from 10:00 p.m. to midnight. I was allowed access to everywhere except the basement. Looking down the dark stairwell into the basement, I felt as if I were missing out and was kind of glad. At one point, while in the lobby, I heard a faint female voice behind me say, "Its okay" then chuckled. When I turned around, I could find no source for the sound.

The hotel has a restaurant, a saloon, a florist shop, and a beauty shop. The lobby is large and impressive. It is decorated with marble, stained glass, gold leaf, and beautiful art work.

Nearby are the Old West tourist towns of Tombstone and Bisbee, Arizona.

Contact Information
1046 G. Avenue
Douglas, AZ 85607
520-364-4481
www.hotelgadsden.com

Jerome Grand Hotel

Another picturesque old mining town in Arizona's southeast desert mountains is the community of Jerome. It is a popular tourist attraction with much to see and a good number of places to stay. The best known of these inns is the Jerome Grand Hotel.

Grand is a befitting name for this massive five-story Spanish Mission style structure. The Jerome Grand Hotel looms over the town of Jerome from its resting spot high upon Cleopatra Hill. From this vantage point one is offered spectacular vistas of the Verde Valley.

The view from my room was the best I enjoyed at any hotel I researched for this book; and that's saying something. The Grand has much more to offer than just a view. It offers beautifully laid out suites, on-site ATV rentals, a gourmet restaurant with an

The Jerome Grand Hotel.

The building's stout construction is evident.

extensive wine cellar, and tours where you can learn about the inn's ghosts. The ghosts come with no extra charge and make a fine mesh with the hotel's haunted history. You can trace most of the spirits here to the building's early days—you see it started off as a hospital.

Built in 1926 and opened early in 1927 as the United Verde Mining Company Hospital, it served northern Arizona and was considered one of the most modern hospitals in the state. Still, people die, even in modern hospitals and the nurses here considered the hospital to be haunted early on.

With its unique architecture, interesting history, and fine reputation, this was a place I was anxious to look over. When checking into the Jerome I requested a haunted room and under the heading of careful what you wish for, they gave me the "Suicide Room." This is the nickname I gave it after I learned of the room's past. The owner said it was their most haunted room. My reply, "Good, thank you." At the time I didn't know the room's history. Another thing about the room is it was next to the suite that used to be the surgery room. While lying there in my bed I couldn't help but wonder how many people spent their last night on earth in this room? What made the experience even more intense was I was the only one checked into the fourth floor that evening, which was something else I wasn't aware of at first. In fact, because of noise in the one room close to me, I assumed others were staying next door. I personally thought I heard the sound of a conversation from the room. I asked at the front desk who had checked into the room. It was then I was advised I was the only person on the top two floors that night.

During the afternoon, while going over some notes in my room, I heard a loud noise in the hall and the transom above the door fell open with a bang. The door started to rattle and the doorknob was turning. I immediately got up to see who was there but when I opened the door I was greeted only by an empty hallway.

During my stay, the elevator lived up to its eerie reputation. It kept moving between floors without any riders in it. In fact, once I heard the elevator move even though it didn't. That's right—I was staring at a stationary cage elevator that was making all the noise of one moving. It was both baffling and creepy. The elevator activity is attributed to the Grand's most active spirit, the ghost of Claude M. Harvey.

Mr. Harvey was a hospital maintenance man. One day during April of 1935, his dead body was found by another hospital employee. Harvey had been working on the building's elevator and it was here he met his death. The elevator moved while he was working on it and pinned his head between the elevator cage and the floor. This broke his neck and killed him. The coroner ruled his death an accident—in just twenty minutes. There was no autopsy and no police investigation. It has been said the mining company didn't want the scandal of a murder and was pushing to sweep things under the rug. Strange too was the elevator was found to be in perfect working order and Claude was known as a good and experienced maintenance man. Some claim he was murdered and the site was made to look like an accident. Another theory was the elevator was tampered with and Claude was murdered that way. Whatever the cause of death, soon afterwards there were reports of orbs and other strange lights being seen in the elevator and its shaft. Also at this time stories started circulating of the elevator moving or at least making the sound of moving even though no one was operating it. This has even been claimed to happen when the building was vacant and no power was on.

Later, another man died in the same room that Harvey did. It was during a time the hospital was closed but still in a stand-by status. The man was the building's caretaker. He committed suicide one night by hanging himself in the boiler room.

At least two other people committed suicide in the building. Both were men who had been patients in Room 32, the room I was staying in. One shot himself. He had been diagnosed with terminal cancer and was told he had only five months to live. He decided not to wait. Another alleged suicide that was supposed to have been committed by a patient of this room was by jumping off the balcony. I say alleged suicide because the man was wheelchair bound, the balcony railing was high, and somehow the wheelchair still went over with the man. Both were found in the parking lot below. Again, there were no witnesses. These days it is said the spirit of one or even both still hang around Room 32 and the hall on that floor. I sort of got that impression during my stay.

This is where they found Claude M. Harvey.

Other areas of activity include the old surgery room that is now a suite. Ether is smelled there. On the fourth floor, a baby is heard to cry in the area where the maternity ward used to be. On the third, the spirit of a little boy named Daniel has been seen. In the lobby a number of employees and the owner all report the doors opening and closing on their own. The switchboard receives calls

These hallways are said to be active with more than just hotel guests.

The town of Jerome, Arizona.

from empty rooms and items are knocked off shelves in the gift shop by an unseen force. One night a desk clerk saw the phantom of a man looking at her from the first landing of the stairs. He stood there staring at her and after a few minutes just faded away.

Other phenomena claimed here are numerous and various types of orbs, phantom footsteps and voices, doors opening and closing by themselves, the smell of cigars where none are being smoked, and electrical appliances operating on their own.

Both now and also early in its history, there have been stories of hearing voices, coughing, moaning, and cries of pain coming from empty rooms. These claims have been made by both patients and personnel from the hospital and both guests and staff from the hotel.

Some have claimed the coughing is from the spirits of people who died of the 1918 flu and then found their way to the building a decade later. It would seem if such coughing spirits existed they would be more likely to have come from the 1920s TB epidemic. The United Verde Hospital did have a TB ward. Also numerous miners would have entered this hospital with any number of lung ailments.

A good number of apparitions have been seen and even photographed. Management has two photos under the glass countertop of the front desk. Curious thing? Look closely at the photo of the white apparition and you will see that it has cast a small shadow near its feet.

The spirit spotted for the longest period is of a bearded old man. He was seen early in the building's history when it was a newly made hospital. A patient was the first to spot him. The old man was gliding down a hall and turning on all the lights as he went. It wasn't long before the nurses started reporting seeing him. Today, guests still report seeing him roaming the halls of the second or third floor. He is usually said to be wearing a plaid shirt and is thought to have been a miner.

Another ghost during its hospital days was a spectral apparition of a woman in a white dress. She would make her appearances on the hospital balcony. It was thought she had been a nurse. She has probably moved on. She hasn't made an appearance since the building opened as a hotel.

The building opened as a hospital in 1927. The fifth floor was added in 1929. The structure is so well built that even though constructed on a steep grade it shows no sign of settling. It is built of poured cement, reinforced with steel. Slag was used as an aggregate. It's stronger than a lot of bunkers I've been in. The lot it's built on had to be leveled first with dynamite.

As with all mining towns, one day the mines closed. For Jerome, that day came in 1950. Most people left town. The mining company closed the hospital but kept it in a mothballed caretaker status just in case of an emergency or if the mines reopened. The hospital stayed this way until 1971. For the next couple of decades it was vacant. In 1994 the building was purchased by the Altherr family. They spent the next two

years repairing the utilities and converting the hospital into a grand hotel. It opened in 1996; the total conversion took a few more years. They did an excellent job.

The lobby has been moved since the hotel first opened and now is where the old service entrance was. There is a gift shop and free hot coffee and tea in the lobby.

The restaurant goes by the interesting name of The Asylum. The food here is excellent and I enjoyed one of the best meals of my trip. The Asylum offers an attractive setting, well-stocked award-winning wine cellar, and a bar to complete the package.

Below the hotel you have the whole town of Jerome. It is full of shops, bars, restaurants, museums, and more. It's a great place to walk around. Keep in mind that you're at 5,300 feet and everything here is either up or downhill. Bring the camera, there is much to photograph. In addition to numerous retail outlets, the town is full of history and additional ghosts. These spirits haunt buildings both occupied and vacant. The list includes two mines, three additional hotels,

The restaurant entrance used to be the emergency room.

a bed and breakfast, a church, a clinic, and many more. Even the restaurant where I had lunch, The Haunted Hamburger, claims to be haunted. A brochure on the table tells the place's story. All I experienced was a delicious cheeseburger.

Contact Information
200 Hill Street
Jerome, AZ 86331
928-634-8200 • 888-817-6788
www.jeromegrandhotel.net

Plaza Hotel

I discovered this location via a billboard. I was driving down the road when I saw a highway advertisement for an old and historic hotel. The sign included a facsimile of the building and its sight just gave me a gut feeling. I went with my gut and it paid a nice dividend.

This hotel is said to be haunted by one of its former owners. The ironic thing is his death saved the building. The past owner, whose spirit refuses to give up the ghost, is said to be of Byron T. Mills. He had been a prominent citizen and businessman. At one time he was the mayor and later the territorial representative. Nowadays his activities are not in a governmental capacity. He returned to his old hotel hanging around a corner of the third floor and the front portion of the first floor.

The front portion of the first floor contains the restaurant, saloon, and lobby. Mr. Mills's ghost has been seen in all these rooms. Pranks, the sound of heavy boots crossing the floor, and the smell of cigar smoke in these areas have also been attributed to him. One story my waitress shared with me had occurred at the table where I was sitting. The restaurant had closed and she had just finished setting the tables when she was called to help in the saloon for a moment. Upon her return to the restaurant she found at three of the tables, including mine, napkins and silverware settings had been tossed onto the floor. She had been the victim of a prank. She just didn't know if it had been Mr. Mills or the other help.

Mr. Mills's favorite haunts are the corners of the third floor where he used to live. He had three or more rooms combined into an apartment and for a few years led a semi-reclusive life there. He still haunts these three rooms today. His favorite now was his favorite then, Room 310.

Later he moved to the Elks Lodge and died there in 1947. At this time the Plaza Hotel was predominately being used as a college dormitory. Mr. Mills had planned to have the place demolished and was even selling off its furniture at the time of his death. His demise saved the building. Instead of being demolished that year, the building continued as a hotel.

The Plaza Hotel.

The adjacent and historic Mercantile Building.

Today Mr. Mills pulls pranks and even puts in the occasional appearance. On the first floor he seems to mostly engage the staff. On the third floor he mostly appears to customers, especially traveling salesmen and women alone in their rooms. Also on the third floor are reports of the sound of heavy boots and the smell of cigar smoke with no apparent sources.

Ever since it was opened in 1882 the hotel's business fortunes have gone up and down like a roller coaster. The first major decline, occurring in 1900, was caused by a combination of an economic depression and a railroad strike. The hotel's fortunes took a major upswing in 1913 when a silent film star, Romaine Fielding, used the hotel as a studio headquarters for his film company. Then in 1915, cowboy, actor, and film director Tom Mix started using the town of Las Vegas and the Plaza Hotel as film sets. The Plaza is also where he stayed while shooting his movies in Las Vegas. After its film career the hotel went back to its roller coaster ride of business fortunes.

The structure faded into a state of decline. In 1982 a group of eighteen local business people formed a partnership to buy and rehabilitate the building. The hotel was thoroughly restored to its former glamour and reopened on December 31, 1982. It is currently listed on the National Register of Historic Places. Recently the hotel has been undergoing an expansion. This was done by buying the old Mercantile Building next door and adjoining it to the Plaza. The Mercantile is also an historic landmark. In fact it seems that every third building in downtown Las Vegas is an historic structure. The downtown shopping district is a piece of living history. The hotel gets its name from the picturesque town square, or plaza, that it anchors.

On my visit management allowed me to roam the place, question staff, check out rooms, and photograph the interior. I tried dinner at their restaurant and enjoyed both the service and the prime rib special. The saloon was full and features live music on weekends. The building exterior is an exquisite Victorian era brick facade. The interior is beautifully restored and contains a number of tin embossed ceilings. The thirty-six rooms are comfortable and well laid out. The hotel has a ballroom and meeting rooms. The expansion will bring more guest rooms, an exercise room, and a gift shop. Management keeps handouts on the hotel's ghost and history behind the front desk.

Contact Information
230 Plaza
Las Vegas, NM 87701
505-425-3591 • 800-328-1882
lodging@plazahotel-nm.com
www.plazahotel-nm.com

The bandstand in the town plaza.

St. James Hotel

Opened in 1872 as a saloon and gambling hall, the Cimarron was as wild a nightspot as any could wish for and more. In fact you might say the place helped put the "wild" in "the wild west." Between 1872 and 1884 no less than twenty-six men died a violent death within the walls of this establishment. Today there is even a list, posted in the lobby, of people who have been killed in the hotel. The hotel was added in 1880, first called the Lambert Inn, later changed to the St. James.

The St. James Hotel.

An old hitching post in front of the hotel.

One of those killed was a gambler named Thomas James Wright. It is claimed he was having an affair with Mary Lambert, the owner's wife. Wright won the hotel in a poker game, but was shot in the back before he could collect on the debt. The leading suspect was Henri Lambert, but no charges were ever filed. After being shot Wright still managed to drag himself into Room 18 where he slowly bled to death. Ever since then he has considered the room his and isn't shy about letting anybody know it. Both customers and employees have been knocked down or shoved back out of the room by either an unseen person or, in one reported case, a glowing orb. Also the chandelier spins around and the lights strobe off and on. With all of this going, the owners decided not to rent the room anymore and just locked it up.

There are at least three other ghosts but they are a lot more pleasant. One is the spirit of Mary Lambert, the wife of the first owner Henri Lambert. The smell of roses, her perfume scent, is known to drift down the second-story hallway. In her old room, Room 17, orbs have been photographed. If you stay in her room and let the window open she'll remind you to close it. You must close it completely or she ends up tapping on it until you close it. She has even woken sleeping patrons up with the noise.

Another ghost has been described as "gnome-like." It is the spirit of a small, pockmarked faced, old man. He likes to pull pranks, particularly on new employees. He seems to enjoy spooking them. He has been blamed for bursting glasses, relighting candles, and moving objects! His apparition has been seen in several places of the hotel. He once appeared on a bar stool and just laughed at some unfortunate new hire. He also takes small items and places them elsewhere in the building.

The last spirit is that of a handsome cowboy. One owner reported seeing the image of a handsome young man wearing a big cowboy hat in a dining room mirror. When the owner turned around there was no one there.

Other phenomenon in the hotel are numerous cold spots located throughout the building, orbs on photos and camcorders, and hotel phones ringing with nobody else on the other end of the line.

On my visit the St. James was closed for a rebuild. It was undergoing a top to bottom reconstruction and a brand new wing was being added. The lobby is retaining its old chandelier and tin embossed ceiling. The hotel and restaurant reopened on June 22, 2009. Only time can tell if the rehab will disturb or drive out the spirits.

Nearby is the ghost town of Colfax, New Mexico. Not much remains of Colfax. Also nearby is the abandoned cemetery of the former mining town of Dawson. Both Colfax and the old Dawson cemetery are reported to be haunted. There is private property around these locations; please be respectful. Close at hand are the Sanore De Cristo Mountains and thousands of acres of national forest land.

Contact Information
Route 1, P.O. Box 2
Cimarron, NM 87714
575-376-2664 • 866-376-2664
www.cimarronnm.com

The hotel sits on one of those roads less traveled.

The Lodge

Perched at an elevation of 9,200 feet overlooking Cloudcroft, New Mexico, is a three-story mountain inn simply named, "The Lodge." This is one of the most written about haunted hotels in America.

The Lodge at Cloudcroft.

The Lodge is said to have more than just one spirit that refuses to give up the ghost. In fact it is said to have four, but the one it's famous for is Rebecca. Rebecca worked as a chambermaid at The Lodge. She was a beautiful, young, flirtatious, vivacious, blue-eyed redhead who easily attracted the attention others. Some claimed she used her beauty to "moonlight" and make extra money. The hotel says she worked there during the 1920s. Other sources claim the 1930s. Whichever, that is also when they claim she was murdered. She had a big, husky boyfriend who worked as a lumberjack. One day he walked in on her to find her in bed with another man. In a jealous rage, he killed them both. Afterwards, he disposed of the bodies and then disappeared himself. Some claim he buried the bodies in the basement of the hotel while others say he disposed of them in the nearby woods. Whichever, the three were never seen again.

These are three of the lost souls who roam the halls of this lofty mountain inn. The fourth is said to be the spirit of a little boy. Rebecca is the most spotted of any of them. She is said to even be flirtatious in death. According to one frightened male guest, he found his bathtub already occupied by a naked, redheaded woman. He called the front desk and insisted someone come up to the room and make her leave. When the clerk arrived the lady had already vanished. Rebecca is said to have been seen by many and usually in a dress of the period. Her favorite room to haunt is Room 101, the Governor's Suite. She likes to play pranks in this room, especially with the phone. Guests in that room frequently get phone calls on the room phone only to have no one on the line. Also the phone from Room 101 will ring the front desk even though no one is in the room. When the help answers at the desk they are only greeted with a dial tone. First you think it's just a bug in the equipment, however, the entire phone system has been changed three times in this hotel and all three systems have had the same problem. The copy machine also seems to have a mind of its own. It has a tendency to turn itself on.

It is also said that the jukebox in the Red Dog Saloon would come on by itself late at night. On my visit I found that the old saloon had been converted into a banquet room with no jukebox in sight.

In addition to the Governor's Suite, Room 109 is said to be active. Claims have been made of lights and the alarm clock turning themselves on, of footsteps outside its door, and of the fan in the bathroom turning itself on and off.

More than one member of the staff told me they came there as non-believers, but after awhile at The Lodge, they now think there may be ghosts after all. One event that turned one employee into a believer involved an older gentleman and his cane. The employee had noticed the man and his cane when he checked in. She said you couldn't help but notice. His cane was very ornate and inlaid with gold. Later the gentleman called the front desk to report his cane missing. The staff immediately started

to search. A few hours later an employee accidentally located it while doing routine maintenance in the tower. She found the cane at the top of the four-story tower, and even more intriguingly she had to unlock the door to enter the structure. How did the cane make it to the top of this secured location?

Photos and newspaper articles of The Lodge's ghost decorate the walls of the resort. Management keeps a journal at the front desk of guest stories and experiences with Rebecca. Photos show orbs, dark shadows, and cascading lights. One interesting note is the claim of shattering glasses. It is said Rebecca only breaks glasses with red wine in them, but never when they contain white wine.

The Lodge opened in 1899. Originally it was used as a boarding house for lumberjacks, tie hacks, and others involved in making railroad cross ties for the Alamogordo and Sacramento Railroad. The Lodge was expanded, and in 1906 opened to the public as a beautiful mountain retreat. On June 13, 1911, The Lodge suffered a devastating fire and was completely rebuilt. This is the lodge you see today. The hotel is open year-round.

The Lodge is not shy about its ghost. In fact they capitalize on it. Rebecca's portrait hangs in the lobby and the saloon is named after her.

During my visit on April 13, I found my room to be nice and the staff even nicer. My dinner, blackberry glazed duck, was one of the best at any of these hotels and the accompanying piano music completed the fine dining experience. The bar, complete with puttied-over bullet holes, came from Al Capone's house. In addition to the saloon and restaurant the hotel has a full service spa, an outdoor pool, gift shop, fitness room, banquet room, and beautiful suites.

For outdoor fun, this is the southernmost ski area of the United States. Also nearby is a golf course at 9,000 feet making it the highest in North America. If you're not accustomed to the high altitude, be careful and take it slowly until your body adjusts to the thinner air. The location is completely surrounded by the Lincoln National Forest.

Contact Information
1 Corona Place, P.O. Box 497
Cloudcroft, NM 88317
575-682-2566 • 800-395-6343
www.thelodgeresort.com

One of the first names for this glorious place was Wonderland. If you've ever been there you understand how it got that name. It was first brought to the attention of the outside world by explorer and mountain man John Colter. He split off from the Lewis and Clark Expedition during its return and spent a winter in Yellowstone. When he finally reached civilization, people refused to believe his stories of boiling mud and buffalo covered in ice.

Located at the intersection of the great western states of Idaho, Montana, and Wyoming, Yellowstone National Park is actually an active volcanic plateau. This is why the region has so many geysers, mud pots, steam vents, and hot springs. In fact there are as many geysers here as there are in the rest of the world.

This also makes the area seismically active. They are still talking about the 1959 earthquake there. And picturesque Yellowstone Lake; it is part of an extremely large volcanic caldera.

The fire season at Yellowstone.

The roads in and to Yellowstone can be crowded, narrow, winding, and frequently closed by fire, landslides, snow, or occupied by wildlife.

This section of the book covers Yellowstone National Park and the towns laying on the approaches to the park. I found six hotels alleged to be haunted in this area. Three are in the park itself and one each in the towns Cody and Moran, Wyoming, and Red Lodge, Montana. I found the hauntings of the three in the park to be more legend than actual history. On the other hand, as you can read for yourself, the three outside the park seemed to be a different story.

The Irma

Well known as the hotel built by William F. (Buffalo Bill) Cody, the Irma is also known for having a few spirits that refuse to hang up their spurs.

Ghosts here include a soldier dressed in a late 1800s army uniform. He has been seen near the bar in the main dining room. Also seen is a spirit thought to belong to Irma, the hotel's namesake and Buffalo Bill's daughter. The apparition is also known as "The Lady in White." She is said to roam the halls of the second floor in the original part of the hotel. Some attribute any unexplained phenomenon to Bill Cody himself. This includes people hearing disembodied voices, even ones that call them by name. This most frequently occurs in the basement.

Other manifestations include glasses shattering or being knocked off shelves or out of people's hands. There are reports of unexplained footsteps, knocking on walls, and other mysterious sounds. Another apparition is that of a lone man. He walks into the main dining room, takes a certain booth, but when a waitress walks over to serve him, he's disappeared.

Another possible spirit might be of a man who was accidentally shot. A man who was celebrating and drinking in the saloon fired a shot into the ceiling and the bullet struck a man sleeping in bed in Room 35. Now the dead man figures it's "his" room. Portraits here get moved to new locations. Staff will make the bed only to find it has been turned

The Irma Hotel.

down before they've even left the room. Guests in this room sometimes complain about the noise coming from the people in the room above them. The only problem is the only thing above them is the roof. Hotel staffers sometimes hear noises from the room while it's supposedly empty. When the employee goes to the room and looks in, the noise suddenly stops. Sometimes this even includes the sound of music and a good number of people in the middle of a party.

Another good story comes from Room 16 and might be more evidence of Irma. Supposedly a guest took a photo of his wife sitting on the room's bed. In the picture is a glowing blue phantom of a woman floating in the air above the bed.

The Irma Hotel was built by Buffalo Bill in 1902 and named after his daughter. He had already helped found the town of Cody, Wyoming, in 1895 and named it after himself. He loved this hotel and maintained an office and two suites for his personal use. The northwest section of the hotel was added in 1929 and the southwest section was constructed in 1976–1977. This part of the hotel is not alleged to be haunted.

Some noteworthy points on the hotel's construction include a number of exterior walls made from locally quarried sandstone and river rock. The old fireplace is made from a collection of rock, ores, minerals, and fossils all from the Big Horn Basin. From early on the hotel went through rebuilds and remodeling but still has kept much of its old-time charm. Some of this old charm includes the Irma's famous long cherry wood bar. The restored suites are beautiful rooms with old-time ambiance. The hotel has a gift shop, lounge, restaurant, and meeting room. Wild West shows are conducted in the street fronting the hotel and the Cody trolley starts its route at the Irma's front door. If that's not enough, you have the rest of downtown Cody laid out in front of you and Yellowstone National Park is just up the highway.

Contact Information
1192 Sheridan Avenue
Cody, WY 82414
307-587-4221 • 800-745-IRMA (4762)
irmahotel@bresnan.net
www.irmahotel.com

This place is the center of activity in Cody.

Lake Yellowstone Hotel

The Lake Yellowstone Hotel, usually just called The Lake Hotel, has the distinction of claiming to be haunted by a former president of United States. President Calvin Coolidge spent most of the summer of 1927 on vacation in the American West. During that time he stayed awhile at The Lake Hotel. He fished a great deal and smoked cigars in the lounge. He would sit in a wicker rocker facing the lake. It was claimed when the hotel was refurbished in the 1980s the rocker was brought out of storage with other furniture from the 1920s and it would rock on its own. Some claim it was Calvin Coolidge enjoying his favorite chair.

The Lake Yellowstone Hotel.

Other stories are of the piano in the lounge playing on its own and of a little boy peering sadly out a window of the vacant fourth-floor attic.

The last alleged ghost, the spirit of Dave Edwards, is another park legend. It is a story of a lonely man and of an empty grave. Mr. Edwards worked for the Yellowstone Lake Boat Company and its owner, E. C. Waters. Mr. Waters is infamous in the park. This is because his treatment of things within the park, from the ships in the boat company to the animals on his island zoo, ranged from neglect to abuse. His treatment of Mr. Edwards seems to have fallen into the neglect category.

Mr. Edwards worked as a summer maintenance man and winter caretaker for the boat company. He lived in a tiny cabin on Stevenson Island. Every day he would row a small boat from the island to the docks at the hotel, do his job, and row back in the evening. On November 12, 1906, Edwards suffered a heart attack and died in his boat on the way back to Stevenson Island. His drifting boat with his body was found later by soldiers from Fort Yellowstone. He was buried near The Lake Hotel. Mr. Waters promised to have the body exhumed in the spring and to have it reburied in Ulta, Iowa. One year after, Mr. Waters was kicked out of the park and the Yellowstone Boat Company sold off. Once again he neglected Dave Edwards and failed to have him reburied.

Mr. Edwards's grave was then neglected and forgotten. Years later when new development took place, Mr. Edwards's grave was paved over. Charles Hamilton, park concessionaire, was building a new store and the access road to it ran right over the burial sight. Mr. Hamilton was supposed to move the whole grave but took the easy way and only moved the tombstone.

The new gravesite was a patch of woods between the hotel and the store. Legend says you can see a light bouncing in the woods at night and that it's the lost soul of Mr. Edwards with a lantern looking for his real grave. On my visit, I found the empty gravesite; sadly it had been vandalized.

During my investigation of The Lake Hotel no one played the piano nor did it play on its own. I did not find any staff member who had any experiences to share and the rocking chair was no longer in the lounge. One thing I found the hotel does have that some people might find scary are bats.

The attic has a colony of them, and periodically their droppings have to be cleaned out.

Yellowstone Lake.

The Lake Hotel is the oldest building in Yellowstone National Park. In fact, other than the Wawona Hotel of Yosemite, it is the longest operating hotel of any national park. Construction started in 1889 and took two years. The doors were opened to the public in the summer of 1891. The original inn was plain, small, and had just eighty rooms to rent.

In the beginning there were two primary ways to reach the hotel. One was by taking a bumpy and dusty stagecoach ride. The other way was by ship across Yellowstone Lake. At 7,733 feet it is the highest navigable body of water in North America. The vessels were the

143

The Yellow Jammer bus.

steamships *Zillah* and *E.C. Waters* and the motorship *Jeann D.* They sailed from 1891 till 1917.

The hotel was remodeled in stages by architect Robert C. Reamer. He had just finished working on the Old Faithful Inn. The Lake Hotel was expanded and rebuilt from 1903 to 1905. This is when the classical columns that distinguish the front of the main building were added. In 1923 the lobby fireplace and another 113 rooms were constructed.

The last Reamer addition was the lounge in 1928. The hotel was closed during 1917 and 1918 for WWI, closed again from 1932 through 1936 because of the Great Depression, and one last time from 1942 through 1945 for WWII. After the Second World War the hotel went through a period of long decline. In the 1970s the Park Service bought the hotel and gave it a ten-year renovation. This is the hotel you see today, however, because of the road layout, you arrive at the back door instead of its grand front entrance.

A special note, you can catch one of the Yellow Jammer tour buses here. These bright yellow, old touring cars have been rebuilt and are a wonderful way to see the park. One of the bus company's early drivers was a Montana cowboy who would later become an actor. His name was Gary Cooper. He drove during the 1923 summer season.

Like most of the major park lodges, The Lake Hotel has a fine restaurant. I had lunch there and the food and service were both excellent. Other services include a post office in the hotel parking lot. I met a buffalo there. I walked around a car and there he was lying on the sidewalk. It took just one snort from him and I forgot about mailing my postcards.

Contact Information
Lake Village Road, Lake Village
Yellowstone National Park, WY 82190
307-344-7311
866-GEYSERLAND (439-7375)
www.travelyellowstone.com

Mammoth Hot Springs Hotel

The Mammoth Hotel is like many hotels in Yellowstone; beautiful, historic, a registered landmark and, according to some, haunted.

It has been claimed that doors lock and unlock by themselves, that keys sporadically fail to work on hotel doors, and that furniture is moved in rooms that have no occupants. Most of these events are supposed to occur on the fourth floor. Although there are theories, it is not known who the spirit is supposed to be. On my research trip to the hotel, I found no evidence of any spirit.

Disappointedly, most of the staff that I interviewed weren't even aware the hotel was alleged to be haunted. There was one exception. A cleaning lady I questioned acknowledged the haunting but refused to talk about. She folded her arms across the chest, stared at the floor, mumbled, and shook her head no.

Still, true danger does lurk the grounds of this hotel. The danger takes the form of large hairy beasts. To be more specific I'm talking about wild buffalo and elk. Most years in Yellowstone National Park there are more injuries or deaths due to animal attacks from these two creatures than from bears and cougars. Buffalo and elk often frequent the hotel grounds and many tourists, judging by accident reports, seem to think they are in an extra-large petting zoo.

The hotel was built in sections starting in 1883. The main lodging section was built in 1911. It was the north wing of the original hotel. Then in 1936 the original

Mammoth Hot Springs Hotel.

hotel, with the exception of the north wing, was completely demolished and replaced. Today's lobby, gift shop, and map room were added in 1937. Cabins were added after that.

The hotel is a complex of cabins, structures, and the four-story main lodge. The hotel and some of its surrounding structures were once part of the U.S. Army headquarters base for Yellowstone Park. In its early history, Yellowstone National Park was protected and administered by the U.S. Army. The army made its headquarters at Mammoth Hot Springs. You can still see this in the architecture and construction of some of the buildings and in the general layout of the area.

The inn offers all the services, attractions, and activities that Yellowstone can provide.

Contact Information
Yellowstone National Park, WY 82190
307-344-7311
866-GEYSERLAND (439-7375)
www.travelyellowstone.com

Don't get this close to elk.

Old Faithful Inn

Old Faithful Inn.

Easily the most famous of all the Yellowstone Park hotels is the Old Faithful Inn. Allegedly it is also the most haunted hotel in the park. There are those who say this world famous inn has three ghosts. One of these ghastly ghosts, the headless bride, is truly a park legend. The story of this phantom has probably been told around more that just a few campfires in the park. The chilling story is about an apparition of a young woman dressed in a flowing white gown. She is seen late at night descending staircases, standing on lobby balconies, or dancing in the crow's-nest. The best part, she carries her head tucked under one of her arms. She is supposed to be the ghost of a bride who was murdered by her new husband on their wedding night. The story claims the newlywed couple checked in during the summer of 1914 and neglected to check out. The girl was but fifteen and the only child of a rich and powerful family in New York City. An older man and a family servant had won her heart while trying to win her inheritance. Her father would have none of it. She refused to listen to her father and married the older man.

The father sent them both packing, expenses paid that is, to be rid of the scandal. The money included a lump sum for the couple to start a new life in the west. During the train trip west, the new groom gambled at cards, but not well. By the time they reached the inn, he had lost all their money. He forced his bride to contact her father and beg for more money, but he refused. When she returned to their room, Room 227, they argued about the situation. The argument ended in her murder. The groom disappeared and the next morning the cleaning lady found the bride's headless body in the bathtub. It is claimed the whole story was made up for tourists by a manager at the inn. Still, it is the most famous ghost story in the park.

A second ghost at the inn is claimed by some to be connected with the headless bride. This is the spirit of a man in his forties or fifties wearing an old style merchant marine uniform. He is said to peer in windows and

Don't get this close to the buffalo.

roam the halls trying various doors. When confronted he is said to simply vanish. Some say he is the runaway groom returning to look for his bride. They theorize that when he ran away he joined the merchant navy and maybe even that his ship was sunk. One note, the sailor's apparition isn't reported until the 1970s. He couldn't have been at sea for sixty years! The time lines don't seem to cross and if the first story is made up anyway, where does our sailor come from?

The third ghost is that of a little boy. He is a lost or deserted child who can't find his parents. His spirit only appears on the second-floor mezzanine and only during the day. His description is around three or four-years-old; three feet tall; wears shorts, tee shirt, and tennis shoes; and speaks with a European accent.

The story is that he makes his presence known by a touch or tug of your clothes from behind. When you turn, you see a little child. He tells you he has lost his mommy or daddy. When you turn away to look for help and then turn back again to speak to the boy, you find that he is gone. Ghost, park

legend, or just a parent's nightmare; who knows?

The inn is a National Registered Historic Landmark and free tours are given daily. It was opened to the public during June of 1904. Most of the material for its construction was obtained within the park. Trees used were mostly Lodgepole Pine and Fir. At first the bark was left on interior wood such as paneling and rails, but it was found to attract too many bugs.

Over the years additional sections have been added and the original part remodeled. Today the inn has 330 rooms. Most of the rooms are small, cozy, and difficult to get. Make reservations. Private baths do not come with all rooms.

The lobby is nothing short of magnificent and is a tourist attraction in itself. The architect, Robert C. Reamer, had said with this lobby he wanted to bring the outdoors inside. He succeeded. The lobby is overlooked by tiered mezzanine and dominated by a massive stone fireplace. High up the chimney is a rather artistic but non-functioning clock. It and the fireplace were put out of action by the 1959 earthquake.

Just outside is the world famous "Old Faithful Geyser." It earned this name because of the regularity of its eruptions. Estimates for the geyser's next eruption are posted in the lobby. More recent seismic activity has changed the regularity of the geyser. Still it is a spectacular sight and a worldwide attraction. So bring your camera and expect crowds.

While you are there, check out the inn's restaurant. The service is friendly, the food is good, and the setting is beautiful. I've always enjoyed my meals there. Besides it's much easier to get a table at the Old Faithful Inn than it is to get a room there.

The inn has a season that extends from early May through the third week of October. Together, the inn and the park offer an A to Z list of facilities and activities.

Contact Information
Yellowstone National Park, WY 82190
307-344-7311
866-GEYSERLAND (439-7375)
www.travelyellowstone.com

Old Faithful Geyser.

Pollard Hotel

The story of this hotel being haunted was passed on to me by the town's newspaper editor along with the request that I check it out for my book. He didn't have all the details but the hotel was claimed by many over the years to have a few ghosts, including one that was said to be of a monkey.

They call the ghost or ghosts here by the name George, no reason, they just do. At least that's the answer the staff gave me. They were exceedingly friendly and also quite helpful. Most had at least one experience they were willing to share. They gave me a personal tour of the facility, then let me roam free and interview guests.

Desk clerks, cleaning crew, and other staff all reported typical events: lights go on or off, trouble with keys "periodically" not working, people get the feeling of being watched while working alone, and more. The usual story was they would clean a room and when they came back to double-check their work, the drapes would be open even though the drapes had been left closed. The same backwards behavior was encountered with lights left off and closet doors left closed. When a member of the staff checked a room many times the light would be on and the closet door open only to have the closet door close itself later that same day.

Strange activity seems to be mostly confined to the north side of the building. The third floor is by far the most active with the

The Pollard Hotel.

exception of an odor of a nineteenth-century perfume in a room on the second floor. The rooms of choice, at least for the ghosts, are 312, followed by 307— the honeymoon suite. In Room 310, the light frequently comes on while the room is vacant. Also on the third floor comes the claim of seeing three quick strobe-like white lights, but only in one's peripheral vision.

One more unique phenomenon is that of smelling smoke in Room 312. This is a no smoking building and no source for the smell is ever located. Strange noises at night in the hotel are blamed on the ghost of the monkey. It is a story told around town. Actually I found very little on this claim. In fact, none of the current staff I interviewed had heard of the monkey story.

The story, and I have only one Internet source for it, is that the monkey was the pet of the second hotel owner's children. One day the pet monkey went missing and was never seen again. It is claimed when the hotel was being rebuilt in the early 1900s, the monkey became trapped behind one of the basement walls. I was able to confirm the

The town of Red Lodge draws lots of tourists.

hotel was rebuilt then and the hotel owner had children; but have found no record of a monkey. If there had been a monkey it is easy to imagine many ways that a crafty, agile, and exotic pet such as a monkey could and would run away. It is hard to imagine how it would have survived its new environment. Such a pet's disappearance, if it ever existed, doesn't seem to be that much of a mystery.

In "it's a small world" category the first guest I interviewed turned out to be from my hometown of St. Louis. We chatted for awhile in the hotel's indoor courtyard. I explained my numerous questions were due to research for a book. During the interview she told me how much she liked the hotel, the staff, and the food in its restaurant. If there had been a video camera, it could have been a commercial for the establishment. She told me she hadn't been aware the place was alleged to be haunted. I asked what room she had stayed in and Room 312 came back as the reply. I told her this was supposed to be the most haunted room in the hotel and asked if she or her husband had experienced anything in the room. She said no, that nothing at all happened, except, well there was this smell of smoke sometimes they couldn't explain. I just smiled and replied, "Oh, really."

The Pollard is a three-story brick structure located on Red Lodge's main business drag. The original hotel was built as the Spofford. It opened for business in 1893 on the 4th of July. In 1902 Thomas F. Pollard bought the hotel, expanded it, and renamed it the Pollard. Among those claimed to have checked in during this hotel's early history are Buffalo Bill Cody, Wild Bill Hickok, Calamity Jane, Jeremiah "Liver Eatin" Johnson, and political firebrand William Jennings Bryan. It and the town of Red Lodge were originally built to service miners and timber men. Over the years, its clientele changed to tourists attracted to nearby Yellowstone National Park.

For a long time the hotel's phone number was simply "1." In 1994 the interior was gutted and the entire hotel was rebuilt. They did a beautiful job. Today the hotel has thirty-nine rooms and suites. Some of these have balconies, fireplaces, and hot tubs. The building has an elevator to ease you on up to the third floor. Besides the upscale restaurant, there is a health club, racquetball courts, and a bar. Breakfast in the hotel's restaurant comes with your room.

Nearby is the ghost town of Washoe, Montana, and the site of the Smith Mine Disaster. The place is said to be haunted by the dead miners. The sad historical marker there will pull at your heart.

Red Lodge is a terminus to one of the most scenic drives in the world, the Bear Tooth Highway. The road is an engineering marvel reaching altitudes of near 11,000 feet.
It offers both white knuckle driving and spectacular vistas.

Contact Information
2 North Broadway
Red Lodge, MT 59068
406-446-0001
800-POLLARD (765-5273)
pollard@thepollard.net
www.thepollard.com

The site of the ghost town of Washoe and the Smith Mine Disaster. It is said to be haunted.

Togwotee Mountain Lodge

In a beautiful mountain pass and sitting on the road to both Yellowstone and the Grand Teton National Parks, the Togwotee Mountain Lodge is well located.

I bumped into this isolated resort while driving in the mountains around Yellowstone. Initially I notice a sign saying, "Gift Shop." So I decided to stop and try to sell some of my books there. Not only did I make a sale, I got to learn about "Bertha." She and her husband had been the first owners of the resort. Only thing is that Bertha has decided to stay on. She is supposed to primarily haunt the annex building. This building contains one of the two gift shops, a convenience store, and the service station of the resort. This used to be the shell of the original lodge. During one of the site's many rebuilds, the original lodge was moved and its site replaced by a parking lot. The old lodge building was moved and converted into the convenience store/gas station.

Staff has reported seeing Bertha's apparition in the moved and reconstructed building. She is also credited with playing with the lights and other more modern fixtures. Some claim she is just being curious. She loved her lodge and is just checking things out. Photos and history of Bertha adorn the walls of the new main lodge. Having bumped into a haunted hotel I didn't want to give up the ghost, so I decided to check in. Even though

The Togwotee Mountain Lodge.

it can't be attributed to Bertha, I did have an interesting experience at the resort.

I was staying on the second floor of the main lodge. After enjoying a good dinner in the restaurant I returned to my room and tried to do some work on the travel log and so forth, but the sound of footsteps running up and down the third floor hall was being a distraction. It sounded like children at play. Try as I might, concentration just wasn't possible with all that racket going on overhead. So I left my room to see what all the racket was about. When I made it to the third floor I found out it was nothing. Absolutely nothing. There was nobody in the third-floor hall. There wasn't even anybody checked into a room on the third floor. It was being remodeled and all the room doors were open. I walked through each room and found nothing to explain the sound. After a toe-tipping search, I returned to my room. After a couple of minutes, the sound started up again. I immediately bolted from my room and ran to the third floor to see if I could catch somebody in the act of doing what I was now doing—running in the hall. Again, all I caught was the sight of an

This was fresh snow and it was late June.

empty hallway. Once again I returned to my room. Once again, after a few minutes wait the noise started up once more. This time I didn't bother to check it out. I just went to bed.

The mountain resort started as a camp in 1921. The founders were Al and Bertha Angle. They named their place Angles Camp. In 1923 they expanded and built a lodge. In the 1950s the Angles sold the lodge to Harry Moll. He sold the business to the Weideman family during the 1960s. The new owners expanded the operation

155

and in 1965 built a new lodge. It is the one you see today. In 1982 the old Angles lodge was moved, renovated, and converted into the convenience store/gas station. Between then and 2002, the resort went through six owners, a number of rehabs, and even a few name changes.

The current owners gave the place yet another expansion, rehab, and name change. The name Togwotee Mountain Lodge had been used before. What was really new was these owners stayed open for the winter. Previously the six-hundred-plus inches of average snowfall was considered a curse. The new owners saw it as a business opportunity. During the winter months the inn provides service for skiers, snowmobilers, and the occasional TV commercial crew.

This lodge comes with a couple of hazards. In fact when you check in, management is good enough to provide their customers with a number of pamphlets dealing with these potential dangers. All the hazards are due to the hotel's location. Sitting as it does in the Togwotee Mountain Pass, it rests at an altitude of 9,658 feet. This can cause altitude

Caution. This is avalanche country!

sickness; be aware of the symptoms. During winter and spring, snow avalanches can be a hazard. The last concern is grizzly bears. This is a major habitat area for them and they are active during the warm months, especially at night. Stay off the trails at night. Make plenty of noise when using them during the day and don't follow my bad example of hiking or mountain climbing solo.

In addition to the rooms at the main lodge building, the resort has fifty-four modern and attractive cabins. Services include the Red Fox Saloon, the Grizzly Steakhouse restaurant, a gift shop, the convenience store combination, and a courtesy computer room.

On-site and nearby activities include horseback riding, hiking, mountain climbing, photography, covered wagon cookouts, whitewater rafting, scenic river float trips, guided fishing tours, guided mountain bike tours, skiing, snowmobiling, and hot air balloon rides. Nearby are Jackson Hole and both the Grand Tetons and Yellowstone National Park.

Contact Information
P.O. Box 91
Moran, WY 83013
866-278-4245 • 800-543-2847
www.togwoteelodge.com

Bibliography

Even western cemeteries were gleaned for information.

These books were used for research on this project. Additional information was also obtained from the Internet, interviews, magazines, newspapers, state historical societies, websites, various museums, pamphlets, and by personally visiting each location.

Branning, Debe. *Sleeping with Ghosts - A Ghost Hunter's Guide to Arizona's Haunted Hotels & Inns.* Phoenix: Golden West, 2007.

Bullock, Seth. *The Bullock Hotel and Unsolved Mysteries.* Deadwood: Dakota, 1993.

Hauck, Denis W. *Haunted Places – The National Directory - Ghostly Abodes, Sacred Sites, UFO Landings and Other Supernatural Locations.* New York: Penguin Books, Revised Edition, 2002.

Kermeen, Frances. *Ghostly Encounters – True stories of America's Haunted Inns and Hotels.* New York: Warner Books, 2002.

Larios, Shellie. *Yellowstone Ghost Stories.* Helena: Riverbend, 2006.

Lewis, Chad and Terry Fish. *The South Dakota Road Guide to Haunted Locations.* Eau Claire: Unexplained Research, 2006.

Munn, Debra D. *Big Sky Ghosts - Eerie True Tales of Montana, Volume II.* Bolder: Pruett, 1993.

Norman, Michael and Beth Scott. *Haunted America.* New York: Tom Doherty, 1994.

Parvis, Sarah. *Haunted Hotels.* New York: Bearfort, 2008.

Sceurman, Mark and Mark Moran. *Weird Hauntings - True Tales of Ghostly Places.* New York: Sterling, 2006.

Scott, David L. and Kay W, Scott. *The Complete Guide to the National Park Lodges.* Gilford: Globe Pequot, 2002.

Terry, Dan. *Missouri Shadows.* Stanton: MO Kid, 2008.

Varney, Philip. *Arizona Ghost Towns and Mining Camps - A Travel Guide to History.* Singapore: AZ DoT, 1994.

About the Author

This is the author resting on part of the film set from the western movie, *Dances with Wolves.*

The author, Bruce A. Raisch, is an adventurer and outdoor enthusiast. He has numerous and varying interests ranging from archaeology to zoology. This combination led to him climbing his first pyramid by the young age of ten. Mr. Raisch has a bachelor's degree in management and is a veteran of the first Gulf War. He has published three other books on the American West, all dealing with old abandoned communities, otherwise known as ghost towns. They are *Ghost Towns of Wyoming*, *Ghost Towns and other Historical Sites of the Black Hills*, and *Ghost Towns of Idaho, the Search for El Dorado.*

To learn more about the author and his three other books, visit his website: www.theghosttownhunter.com.